John Campbell

**Candid and Impartial Considerations on the Nature of the Sugar Trade**

The comparative importance of the British and French islands in the West-Indies: with the value and consequence of St. Lucia and Granada, truly stated

John Campbell

**Candid and Impartial Considerations on the Nature of the Sugar Trade**
*The comparative importance of the British and French islands in the West-Indies: with the value and consequence of St. Lucia and Granada, truly stated*

ISBN/EAN: 9783337318598

Printed in Europe, USA, Canada, Australia, Japan

Cover: Foto ©Suzi / pixelio.de

More available books at **www.hansebooks.com**

CANDID AND IMPARTIAL

CONSIDERATIONS

On the NATURE of the

SUGAR TRADE.

CANDID AND IMPARTIAL
CONSIDERATIONS
On the NATURE of the
SUGAR TRADE;
THE
COMPARATIVE IMPORTANCE
OF THE
BRITISH and FRENCH ISLANDS
IN THE
WEST-INDIES:
WITH
The VALUE and CONSEQUENCE of
ST. LUCIA and GRANADA, truly stated.
Illustrated with COPPER-PLATES.

LONDON:
Printed for R. BALDWIN in Paternoster Row.
MDCCLXIII.

Candid and Impartial

# CONSIDERATIONS

ON THE

Nature of the Sugar-Trade, &c.

THERE cannot be any thing more worthy of a good citizen in a free state than to study public affairs with candour and assiduity. It is his privilege, it is his birthright to apply himself to the knowledge of those things, which as they belong to all, ought to be the care of all, and in order to this all ought to understand them. In a free country every man who is properly qualified may be called to take a part in government, and therefore every man who finds he has talents requisite to such inquiries should pursue them, that whenever occasion offers, or his duty requires, he may be in a capacity to serve his country; that is, to serve it effectually, with utility to the common-weal, and with honour to himself. For these are circumstances inseparable, and the public must be usefully served, otherwise a man cannot be said, or be conscious to himself, of having served the public with honour.

It may be truly affirmed of this, as of every other virtuous and honest employment, that a man finds his interest combined with his duty. The study of public affairs enlarges the mind, strengthens the faculties, and extends all the powers of his understanding. It was this, that elevated the great men of antiquity to that height of reputation, and made them seem not only equal, but even superior to the most exalted stations. It enabled them and will enable us, if prosecuted with due application, to judge of things from our proper lights, to have opinions of our own, and consequently to be out of the reach of imposition, which is the only method that leads to steadiness in conduct, and to an invariable pursuit of our own interests, by promoting those of our country. This is rational and intelligible patriotism, by which the happiness of the individual, springing from the welfare of the public, he never can be tempted to digress from the right road, or be flattered with the foolish hopes, of aggrandizing himself or his family, at the expence of his country, which this study will convince him, is a practice as weak as it is wicked.

As the turning mens minds to the consideration of such things, would be profitable to the state; so it would at the same time be useful and

and serviceable to government. The views of an administration can only, in the opinion of sensible people, procure it either the denomination of good or bad; and as the welfare of the state must be the sole object of an upright administration, it is impossible that such a one, should distaste or discourage such studies, or, to speak with greater propriety, should not esteem and cherish them.

A good administration can derive its stability from nothing else, for they will be best supported by those, by whom their designs are best understood. If then, the generality of the nation, or at least the men of family and fortune, bend their thoughts this way, and become thereby both able and candid judges of their conduct, ministers who mean well, can never have any thing to fear. Factions take their rise, and are strengthened from impositions on weak understandings, and have always a bias to luxury and licentiousness, because they divert the thoughts of men, from the serious consideration of their true interests to the gratification of their humours or their passions; but if the real, certain, and permanent sources of national happiness, were closely and candidly examined into, and clearly and thoroughly understood, there would be no room left for these delusions, and the nation, feeling its own felicity, would fear nothing so much, as an alteration in its circumstances; and a change of those measures, from which so many benefits had been derived.

There is no doubt, that this kind of knowledge requires some labour, and much attention; that many enquiries are necessary, in order to obtain the proper lights; that some pains must be bestowed in comparing them, and in digesting clearly those informations we receive from them. But these obstacles arise in discovering truths of every kind, and the pleasure that is derived from overcoming them, is never more sensible or satisfactory, than in respect to such truths, as regard political concerns. By this means, we avoid passing harsh and hasty judgments, on subjects of very great importance, and a little time and patience is certainly well bestowed, in examining things of consequence to the public, and in deciding with discretion, where ourselves and our posterity are so deeply interested in the event, and must either prosper or suffer so much, from the justice or injustice of the decision.

It seems at present, to be thought a point of great importance, and worthy of being fully discussed, whether the island of *Granada* and its dependencies, be a just, that is a full equivalent, for the island of *St. Lucia*? In order to discover this, it is not barely necessary, to gain as distinct a knowledge of each of these islands, as it is possible; but there are also many other things, that ought to be previously known, in order to make the comparison between them with propriety; and more especially, we ought to have for this purpose, a just or at least a general

neral idea of the nature and importance of the sugar trade, and a clear conception of the true state of those, that have been hitherto stiled the *Neutral Islands*. For without making these previous inquiries, it is not possible to discern the consequences, that may with probability be expected to follow, from this exchange, and yet it is from the prospect of these consequences alone, that the propriety or impropriety of this exchange, can be certainly determined.

The CANES, which produce that sweet liquor of which SUGAR is made, grow in all the four quarters of the globe, and in three of them, spontaneously. They were certainly known to the ancients, though what we call sugar, was not; for the manufacturing the sweet juice of the cane, into that form, was the invention of the *Arabians*, who bestowed upon it the name it bears, calling it in their own language *Succar*. It was brought by the *Moors* into *Spain*, and cultivated by them, with the greatest success, in the kingdoms of *Granada*, *Valencia*, and *Murcia*. In the two last, it is made in great perfection, though not in great quantities, at this day; for though it is computed, that the *Spaniards* import to the value of at least a million of pieces of eight, in *Foreign* sugars, yet this is owing entirely to an error in government, and the insupportable Tax of thirty-six *per Cent.* which has already reduced their sugar works very low, and notwithstanding all the remonstrances that have been made upon this subject, may very probably in process of time put an end to them.

About the beginning of the fifteenth century, the *Spaniards* introduced the manufacture of Sugar, and very probably the canes, into the *Canary* Islands, where they throve exceedingly; producing great wealth to the inhabitants, as well as a very large revenue to the crown. In 1420 the Infant Don *Henry* of *Portugal*, the great promoter of discoveries, directed *sugar canes* to be carried from the island of *Sicily*, to that of *Madera*, where they prospered so happily, as that within a district of nine miles, in compass, the *fifth* which that prince reserved to his military order, amounted to *fifteen hundred* hogsheads of Sugar, each of a thousand weight; and consequently the whole produced *seven thousand five hundred* such hogsheads; which in those early times, and when the vessels employed in trade were so small, was thought, and with great reason, a very considerable improvement.

The same nation, having discovered and begun to plant the country of *Brazil* in *America*, turned their thoughts to the cultivation of the *sugar canes*, which they found naturally growing there, and prosecuted their endeavours with such effect, that chiefly from the profit they derived from this commodity, they began to form to themselves very extensive views; believing that from the advantages of situation, climate, soil, and rivers, they might be able to carry

their

their commerce higher than any other nation; to which prediliction in favour of *Brazil,* some authors of good authority have ascribed the decline of their affairs in the *East Indies.* But these hopes, whether well or ill grounded, were frustrated, by the invasion of the *Dutch.* The *Spaniards* having the like views with the *Portugueze,* by the direction of *Ferdinand* the *Catholic,* carried sugar canes from the *Canaries* to the island of St. *Domingo,* where they were first planted, by *Pedro de Atenca,* and the first sugar mill was erected by *Gonzales de Velosa,* in 1506. But finding the natives unfit for these labours, they introduced *Negro* slaves, and thus we have traced the history of this commodity and manufacture, which had flourished from time immemorial in the *East,* to its introduction in the *West* Indies.

At what time SUGAR was first brought into *England,* it is difficult to say; but that it was in common use in 1466, appears from the record we have of the feast given by Dr. *George Nevil,* when he was installed archbishop of *York,* where it is said, there were spices, *sugared delicates,* and wafers plenty. In that very old treatise entitled the *Policy* of *keeping* the *Sea,* the author inveighing against the useless things brought by the *Venetians* from the *Indies,* adds that they furnished but very few of the *necessaries* of *life* except *sugar.* In succeeding times, we had this commodity as may be collected from our old writers upon trade, from *Spain, Sicily,*

*Sicily*, *Portugal*, *Madera*, *Barbary*, and other Places; which as the Use of it increased, may very probably be supposed, to have created a desire of obtaining some country for ourselves, in which it might be cultivated, in a degree sufficient for our consumption.

The famous Sir *Walter Ralegh* by his Voyages to *South America* in the reign of queen *Elizabeth* and king *James*, had raised so high an opinion of the riches of *Guiana*, that after his unfortunate death, the project of planting that country was pursued by Sir *Olyff Leigh*, who sent his brother thither, and afterwards by other gentlemen, who at length desisting from their pursuit of gold and silver, were content to form plantations there, and after occupying and deserting several places, at length fixed upon the mouth and banks of the river *Surinam*; which though very little notice has been taken of it by our writers, seems to have been the first *sugar* colony we ever had, and to have grown by degrees to more importance, than perhaps it has been judged proper to preserve in remembrance, as this country was ceded to the *Dutch* by the treaty of *Breda*. It may however be proper to take notice, in support of what has been said, that it appeared a few years before it was given up, to have had *sixty thousand* inhabitants, two thirds of which were whites, who made there great quantities of sugar, ginger, indigo, and cotton, and by allowing all nations to live and trade there freely, without any civil, religious,

or

or commercial reſtraint, employed about two hundred ſail of ſhips, amounting in the whole to upwards of fifteen thouſand ton. But tho' the country was given up, it was ſtipulated, that the people ſhould have full liberty to withdraw with their effects, and in conſequence of this, the greateſt part of the *Engliſh* retired to ſome or other of our plantations.

According to ſome accounts, a ſhip ſent by Sir *Olyff Leigh* to the country of *Guiana*, firſt touched at *Barbadoes*. But according to others, this iſland was diſcovered by a ſhip of Sir *William Curteen*'s returning from *Fernambuco* in *Brazil*, about the beginning of the laſt century. It afterwards as we ſhall more than once have occaſion to mention, was granted by king *Charles* I. by Patent dated *June* 2d, 1627, to the earl of *Carliſle* together with other Iſlands, upon pretence that he had been at great expences in ſettling them. The inhabitants ſpent near forty years, in raiſing indigo, ginger, cotton, and tobacco; and then bethought themſelves of ſugar canes, which were brought hither from *Braſil*, and this in the very ſhort ſpace of *ten* years, ſo changed their affairs, that the planters from being poor, grew to great opulence, and either importing or purchaſing great numbers of *Negroes* from *Africa*, extended their plantations, not more to their own emolument, than to that of their mother country, and it was owing to the ſudden and ſurpriſing fortunes they made, that the value of the ſugar trade came to be be underſtood and cheriſhed, as one of the moſt beneficial in which the *Engliſh* had ever engaged. In conſequence of *which* ſeveral of the moſt eminent planters were by king *Charles* II. created *baronets*, that it might appear the temple of honour was open to thoſe, who added to the ſtrength of the nation, by improving the arts of peace, as well as to ſuch who ſignalized themſelves in her defence, in a time of war.

Thoſe who were ſettled in our other iſlands, led by the example of the people of *Barbadoes*, introduced the manufacture of *ſugar* likewiſe into them, and *Jamaica* being added to our dominions, produced a vaſt augmentation of ſugar territory; ſo that during the latter moiety of the laſt century, we greatly exceeded all the other nations, who had hitherto dealt in this commodity, and no new formidable rivals as yet appearing, we carried it on with ſuch advantage, as to export great quantities of ſugar, even into thoſe countries, from which we had imported this commodity heretofore; particularly into the *Levant*, where by ſelling our ſugars cheaper than they could make them, all the plantations formerly ſettled in the *Turkiſh* dominions gradually declined, and, except in *Egypt*, at laſt wore out. But in conſequence of our making ſuch immenſe quantities of ſugar, it became requiſite to take every method of promoting its conſumption at home, in order to the ſupport of our colonies, the foreign market having only a certain extent, the commodity

was

was in danger of becoming a drug if this expedient had not been found to keep up its price; this however clearly shews, what a mighty change was made in our circumstances, in respect to this very valuable article of commerce.

The *French* came somewhat later than we, into these parts of the world, as will appear even from their own writers, and were not so early in making sugars, though they found the canes actually growing in the island of *Martinico*, nor did they make any great progress, for many years after they began to plant sugar; notwithstanding they had the assistance of many of the *Dutch*, who took shelter in their islands, after the *Portugueze* drove them out of *Brazil*. This was owing to a great variety of causes; but more especially to most of their islands remaining a long time in private property, being transferred from one proprietor to another; their desire of grasping more islands than they could occupy; their depending too much upon a military force, and their not having a sufficient number of *Negroes*. Many of these errors were corrected in time; but then they had new difficulties to struggle with, so that after all, though they did proceed, they proceeded but slowly, and made little or no figure in the sugar trade, till after the conclusion of the treaty of *Ryswick*, when the nature and consequences of commerce, began to be thoroughly understood, and vigorously prosecuted, under the auspice of COLBERT, who wisely considered the acquisition

quifition of trade, as a more folid foundation for power, than the acquifition of territory, and who was very careful in drawing his lights, from the moft experienced merchants, not only in *France* but in all the other countries in *Europe,* which he again farther improved by fubmitting all the informations they gave to the ableft politicians.

The acquifition of part of *Hifpaniola,* was another very great, though not an immediate advantage to the *French,* for they acquired it gradually, and not without confiderable refiftance, which as it hindered them from planting, fo it prevented, at leaft in a great meafure, the apprehenfions that otherwife would have arifen, from fo great a conqueft. After they had effectually fixed themfelves there, they quitted their fugar plantations in the ifland of *Tortuga,* which had fucceeded very well, but appeared infignificant in comparifon of what was expected from *St. Domingo,* to which the inhabitants removed. The war on account of the fucceffion to the crown of *Spain,* gave a temporary check to their improvements; but at the fame time, it was beneficial to them in another point of view, as it delivered them from any farther difputes with the *Spaniards,* and tho' we were already jealous of the progrefs of their fugar colonies, yet we were fo much occupied by the war in *Europe,* and the efforts we made in *America,* were fo indifferently conducted, that though they did fuffer, yet ftill they fuffered much

lefs

less than otherwise they might have done, if we had been more attentive to our own interests, and to the favourable opportunity we then had, of effectually preventing them from becoming, as they have since been, our most formidable rivals. By the treaty of *Utrecht* indeed, we acquired the cession of those quarters which they possessed in the island of *St. Christophers*. But the *French* Planters removed from thence into their other islands, and as they did not want land, this cession of their part of *St. Christophers*, was no disadvantage to them, though it has certainly proved a very considerable benefit to us.

From the conclusion of the peace of *Utrecht*, they have been much more attentive to their interests in this particular, have thriven accordingly, and have had many other incidental advantages. Their islands were full of people, when they began to set in earnest about their sugar plantations. Their government has been very attentive to their interests, more especially in point of duties, which notwithstanding all the exigencies of their state, have ever continued low; which has been a great encouragement to their planters. Besides this, many wise regulations have been made in respect to sending white people, as well as black, and great encouragements have been given, not only for the support of their industry, but also for supplying them with negroes. But possibly with all these advantages, they never could have carried

their

their improvemements so high, if it had not been for the assistance given them, by the inhabitants of our northern colonies, in taking off their Rum and Melasses, which was a benefit their own government could not give them, and a detriment to us, which though early discerned and loudly complained of, never could be effectually redressed.

The *Dutch* came first into *America* with an armed force, and with a strong fleet attacked *Brazil,* being in the hands of the *Spaniards,* who were at that time masters of *Portugal;* made a great impression there in 1624, which they prosecuted with such effect, that they became masters of *six* of the *fourteen* captainships, into which that country is divided, which they held about thirty years, and in which they made annually about *twenty-five thousand* chests of sugar. After the *Portugueze* had thrown off the *Spanish* yoke, they endeavoured to expel the *Dutch* from *Brazil,* which at length in consequence of the long war, the republic had with the *English,* they accomplished, though the cession was not made, till the year 1661, when amongst other advantageous articles, the states obtained the sum of *eight* millions of florins, which they condescended to take in sugar and other merchandize, under the title of an *equivalent.* In the first *Dutch* war in the reign of *Charles* the *second,* they took from us the country of *Surinam,* which was ceded to them in exchange for *New York,* by the Treaty of *Breda* in 1667, and that cession

cession confirmed by the treaty of *Westminster* in 1674, during which period and for some time after, that is, till the *French* king suppressed his *West India* company, the *Dutch* availed themselves of most of the sugars made in the *French* islands, in which commerce they are said to have employed an hundred sail of ships. To their colony of *Surinam* they have now added *Brebecie* and *Isaquepe* upon the same continent, and though the whole of this country is very marshy and unwholsome, yet they are thought to make a quantity of sugar there, not much inferior to what they brought from *Brazil*, while it remained in their hands.

Besides these colonies which are on the continent of *South America*, they have likewise the islands of *St. Eustatia* and *Curaçoa*, &c. places that would be very insignificant in the hands of any other nation; but as they manage them, they are very advantageous. For being a kind of free ports, to which the ships of all the *European* nations resort, they avail themselves in time of peace, by a smuggling trade to a very large amount; and in time of war, they are still greater gainers by a contraband commerce. The vast magazines of all kinds of *European* and *East-India* goods, which they have constantly well supplied in these isles, and the conveniencies they afford to the ships of all nations, that resort to them, for the sake of trading with each other, for commodities and in a manner not permitted any where else, brings them at all times a great *resort*

*sort* of vessels, by which the *Dutch* inhabitants are vastly enriched, and by keeping their duties low, and taking the advantage of all sorts of trade, they send home very considerable returns annually.

But besides all this, they have always drawn and still continue to draw immense advantages, from their art in refining sugar, particularly at *Amsterdam*, to which port they brought amazing quantities formerly, not only from *Barbary, Portugal,* and *Madera,* but also from the *Levant* and *Egypt,* as they still do, from their own colonies, from *England, France, Brazil,* and when it can be done with profit, from their settlements in the *East Indies,* particularly in *Java,* where they make vast quantities. These refined sugars, by means of the great rivers in *Germany,* the *Weser,* the *Elbe,* the *Rhine,* the *Mein,* and the *Moselle,* they vend through all that extensive and populous country, and exchange them for various kinds of raw commodities, which are afterwards manufactured in their own provinces, and thus by their perpetual attention to the wants of all their neighbours, their dexterity in turning those wants to their own advantage, their indefatigable industry, and the cheapness of their navigation, they are much greater, and also much surer as well as more constant gainers by sugar, than is generally imagined, or if this matter was more fully explained, would be easily credited.

The

The *Danes* have been long in possession of *St. Thomas*, an isle that lies the most to the west of any of those that are stiled the *Virgins*. It is in truth, little more than a very high mountain, with a narrow skirt of flat ground round it, not quite twenty miles in circumference, but with a tolerable good port, and that when once entered, safe and commodious. The use they formerly made of this island was much the same, that the *Dutch* still make of *St. Eustatia* and *Curaçao*; that is, they admitted ships of all nations, and took no exceptions at any kind of trade. In this they went even beyond the *Dutch*, or rather, the *Dutch* carried on in this *Danish* port that sort of commerce with privateers, which they did not think it quite so safe to carry on in their own; and by this means left the odium of such practices upon the *Danes*, and drew the profit arising from thence to themselves. But things are now quite altered. When the *French* quitted *Santa Cruz*, which lies five leagues from *St. Thomas*, the *Danes* entered into possession of that island, which is much more considerable in extent, being thirty miles long, and nine or ten broad; and though there are eminencies, yet there are no mountains. Upon those rising grounds they have abundance of different sorts of fine timber; but the water is bad, and the air unwholsome. Both these islands were in possession of the *Danish West India* company till very lately, when his present *Danish* majesty, having bought up their actions, dissolved

ved that company, and gave every sort of encouragement that could be devised or desired, for the improvement of these small islands. In consequence of this, the sides of the great mountain in the before-mentioned small isle of *St. Thomas*, are at this time so thoroughly cultivated, that it yields between two and three thousand hogsheads of sugar annually, and this last-mentioned island of *Santa Cruz*, under all its disadvantages, is in a very fair way of being also very compleatly planted, though chiefly by *British* subjects, and by this means *Denmark* will be fully supplied with sugar for the future, and will also have some to spare for foreign markets.

By thus tracing succinctly the history of sugar, or rather the trade in sugar, we see through how many different hands it has passed. We may also without any great difficulty discern the causes that have produced those alterations. It will from hence appear, that it is not the bare power of cultivating the canes, which is very practicable in different parts of *Europe*, and it has been shewn that they grow naturally in the three other parts of the globe; nor yet the skill of manufacturing it, which will preserve this trade to any one nation. From thence it follows, that the hopes of monopolizing sugar, and in consequence of this, selling it at an advanced price, is a mere commercial chimera, the very attempting of which, would very probably transfer it back to some of its former possessors, seffors, or, which is full as likely, fix it effectually in the hands of the inhabitants of *Holland*, who owe their fuccefs in commerce to their fteady adherence to a very fimple and plain maxim, That thofe who can fell the beft commodity cheapeft, will always command the market.

There might be many more points of great utility, deduced from a larger hiftory of this very lucrative commerce, but attempting that would too much fwell this little work, in which what has been faid, was principally with a view to introduce a very fuccinct enumeration of the advantages that arife to us from the fhare we have in the fugar trade. For without having a general idea of the whole, it is fimply impoffible to judge with any degree of certainty or precifion of any of its parts, as the particular benefits that arife from them are chiefly derived from the relation they bear to the whole, and therefore the fureft as well as the cleareft way of rendering thefe vifible, is to point out and illuftrate the feveral circumftances by which our *fugar colonies* prove in various refpects ferviceable to *Great Britain*, and thereby amply repay the protection they receive from, and at the fame time merit the continual attention, that for her own fake ought to be paid by them to their mother country. For without thoroughly underftanding and keeping conftantly in our minds this natural, this infeparable connection of interefts, we fhall be liable to continual miftakes, as in truth all the errors into which we have ever fallen, in this respect, has been owing to no other cause than that of supposing, in consequence of some plausible pretences, that there might be a difference between the interests of this nation in those colonies, and the interests of our countrymen settled in those colonies, which can really never happen; so that in consequence of our being deceived by such appearances, the wrong measures into which we have been so deceived, have been always equally dangerous, and in some instances fatal to both.

The inhabitants of those of our *American* islands, which from their principal commodity, or rather manufacture, are denominated the *sugar colonies*, are composed of *Whites* and *Blacks*, or in other words of *British* subjects and *African* slaves. It is from the skill and industry of the former, supported by the painful and indefatigable labour of the latter, that not sugar only, but various other commodities also to an immense value, are raised in those countries, and exported to different parts of the world. It is to the cheapness of the labour of these poor people, who likewise procure from thence the greatest part of their own subsistence, that those costly and extensive works, which are necessary in a sugar plantation, are derived, as well as all the other necessaries that it requires, and whatever else contributes to the support, conveniency, and the affluence of our countrymen in these isles, who are their masters; and indeed,

deed, it is to this circumstance of the cheapness of their labour, that the sugar trade with regard to *Europe* at least, is in a great measure confined to *America*, as on the other hand, its being confined to *America*, is the principal cause of its affording such a variety of advantages, and more especially of its contributing so highly to the support of navigation, and in consequence of that to the maintainance of naval power; from these general outlines of the importance of our sugar colonies, we will, for the sake of perspicuity, enter a little more minutely into the branches of their commerce with *Great Britain*.

These so necessary *Negro* slaves are purchased in *Africa* by the *English* merchants with a great variety of woollen goods; a cheap sort of fire arms from *Birmingham*, *Sheffield*, and other places, powder, bullets, iron bars, copper bars, brass pans, *British* malt spirits, tallow, tobacco-pipes, *Manchester* goods, glass beads; some particular kinds of linens, ironmonger and cutlery ware, certain toys, some *East India* goods, but in the main, with very little that is not of our own growth or manufacture. Besides these slaves, which make up the greatest part of their cargo, our *African* traders also purchase gold, elephants teeth, and dying woods, with some valuable drugs; and in the *West Indies* also, when they have any surplus of slaves, they dispose of them at a very high price to foreign nations, by which there has been formerly very

large

large sums got, and all returned to *Great Britain*. When these *Negroes* are sold to the *British* planters, they cannot be employed in or furnished with instruments proper for their daily labour, but with fresh advantage to the *British* nation.

For in his field work the planter must supply his *Negroes* with bills, hoes, axes, iron chains, and other necessary tools, which in consequence of their being continually used, makes it necessary to have yearly supplies for the making good *wear* and *tear*, which in that moist and sultry climate especially, rises to a very considerable amount. To this we may add, that these poor people living very hard, and selling no small part of the provisions they raise, lay out constantly the little product that thus arises out of their industry, which they are allowed to retain, with such as are stiled *Negro* traders, chiefly for *Birmingham*, *Sheffield*, and *Manchester* wares, so that all this, which, their number considered, amounts to no despicable sum, is likewise returned hither, which is the rather mentioned to shew, that if any means should be devised to render their condition more tolerable, and their circumstances more easy, the fruits of their own labour, as well as that employed in their master's service, would all necessarily center in this island.

But the field expences are trifling, in comparison of the utensils necessary in the sugar works, such as coppers, mill cases, ladles, skimmers, mills, ftills, and almoft numberlefs other articles, to which may be added nails, locks, hinges, bolts, and lead, employed by the planter in his other buildings, and the almoft innumerable kinds of iron work that are ufed in waggons, carts, mill works, and other things not only exceedingly expenfive at the firft fetting out, but which from their being in continual ufe, conftantly wear out and require frefh fupplies. All thefe, at whatever price, muft be had from *Britain*, and even the lumber, that is timber, cattle, *&c.* though it comes from the northern plantations, is paid for by fugar planters, and goes in difcharge of the *balances* refpectively due from thofe colonies to *Britain*; or at leaft a very great part of them, are this way difcharged.

To thefe we muft add, moft of the materials neceffary for building their houfes, by far the greateft part of their furniture; and it is not only by their induftry and the fuccefs attending it, that *Britain* is enriched, but alfo by their luxuries, whenever they are in a condition to have more than the conveniences of life, fuch as coaches, chariots, chaifes, together with all forts of wearing apparel, and no fmall part even of their provifions, fuch as cheefe, bacon, pickles, beer, ale, and cyder in vaft quantities, and flour and bifcuit when they are cheap. Their *Negroes* alfo, are in this refpect very beneficial, for flight as their cloathing is,

C 4 they

they consume vast quantities of check linnen, striped hollands, fustian, blankets for their bedding, long ells and bays for warm cloathing, coarse hats, woollen caps, cotton and silk handkerchiefs, knives, razors, buckles, buttons, tobacco pipes, fishing tackle, small glasses, thread, needles, pins, and innumerable other articles, all of *British* growth or manufacture. As the demand for all these is limited only by the means of acquiring them, it is from thence self-evident, that in proportion as these colonies thrive, the supplies from *Britain* continually augment, so that whatever would contribute to increase the prosperity of either white or black inhabitants in these islands, would at the same time necessarily extend and enlarge the *British* commerce.

But we must not forget, that as sugar, rum, and molasses, so likewise cotton, indigo, pimento, mahogany, fustic, and, in a word every thing that comes from these plantations are bulky commodities; they require and employ an immense quantity of shipping, the freights of which outward and homeward-bound, insurance, commissions, and petit charges, are all paid by the inhabitants of these islands, and are all received by *British* merchants and factors, and in respect to these also, as much as they can be more extended the greater will the benefit be that *British* subjects must acquire from them, in consequence of that wise law, by which all that arises from the produce of these *British* colonies,

colonies, is effectually secured to *Britain*. We must also take into this account the very large revenue which annually arises from this commerce to the crown, and which if that commerce can be any ways enlarged, will also reap from thence a continual augmentation.

If upon the whole we attentively consider, that industry only ought to be accounted the real wealth of a nation, and that it is not either the fertility of soil, the excellence of climate, or even the number of people, if those people are not usefully employed, that can give strength to a state, or bestow peace and independence upon individuals, upon which however their happiness must always depend: If we revolve in our minds, what an amazing variety of trades receive their daily support, as many of them did originally their being, from the calls of the *African* and *West India* markets: If we reflect on the numerous families of those mechanics and artisans which are thus maintained, and contemplate that ease and plenty, which is the constant as well as just reward of their incessant labours: If we combine with these, those several tribes of active and busy people, who are continually engaged in the building, repairing, rigging, victualling, and equipping, the multitudes of seamen who earn their wages by navigating, and the prodigious crowds who likewise obtain their bread, by loading, unloading, and other necessary attendances upon ships: If we remember, that the subsistence of all these ranks and degrees of men, thus usefully employed, constitutes a new fund of support to the landed and trading interests of this country, that their various consumptions contribute to raise the value of land, to cause a regular and constant demand for immense quantities of our native commodities, as well as to procure a vent for our numberless manufactures, and that all this is equally regular, permanent, and certain; we may from thence form a competent idea of the prodigious value of our *sugar colonies*, and a just conception of their immense importance to the grandeur and prosperity of this their mother country, to whom from the circumstance of this relation, they pay without repining such prodigious tributes.

The usual method of treating such subjects as these, in order to place them in the strongest and most striking light, has been to reduce the profits of the particular branch of commerce considered under some degree of calculation, in which however as there is necessarily some part, and too often a great deal of supposition, and many things asserted the truth of which (though really so) it might be very difficult, if not impossible to prove; men of critical judgments, very frequently disregard them. Yet it is hoped, that all circumstances considered, what follows with respect to the island of *Barbadoes*, the oldest of our present *West India* sugar colonies, will be allowed to be rather much below,

low, than any thing beyond the truth. Let us then exclude all that accrued from it to the people of *England* before the restoration, and estimate its produce from one thousand six hundred sixty, to seventeen hundred and sixty, at sixteen thousand hogsheads of sugar, which make twelve thousand ton annually, and omitting entirely the rum or spirits, molasses, cotton, ginger, aloes, and all the other commodities of the island, estimating this at twenty pounds a ton, it will amount to two hundred and forty thousand pounds *per annum*, or twenty-four million sterling, in the course of the century either gained or saved to this nation, which, considering that *Barbadoes* is not bigger than the *Isle of Wight*, must appear a most amazing sum; and yet in proof of the modesty of this computation, it would be easy to name a very intelligent author, who before the close of the last century, affirmed that no less than thirty millions had been gained by our possession of *Barbadoes* at the time he wrote. But though his zeal might possibly carry him a little too far then, there is not now the least room to question, that the very best judges, by which is to be understood those who are best versed in these kind of things, and who also best understand this trade, would more readily concur in fixing the amount of our profits, during the period before assigned, at thirty than at twenty-four millions.

To conclude this part of our defign with a few general obfervations, which from what has been already faid, cannot but be clearly and fully comprehended.

In the firft place then, the old objection, which from an appearance of truth had fome degree of weight before this fubject was thoroughly underftood, that people going to our plantations weakened the mother country, is now, from our better acquaintance with the fubject, inconteftably obviated. For thofe who go thither, do it either from a principle of neceffity, or with a view to the making their fortunes. In the firft cafe they could not, and in the fecond they would not ftay at home. So that when we confider attentively the confequences of their going to the plantations, that is the confequences of their going thither, with refpect to *Britain*; inftead of looking upon fuch people as loft, we ought to confider them as preferved to this country, which but for our plantations they would not have been. For furely the cafe is much better with refpect to this nation, in regard more efpecially to the inhabitants of the northern part of this ifland, who repair now in fuch numbers to our colonies, than when they were fcattered through *Ruffia*, and even throughout *Afia*, as mechanics, fupplied *Sweden*, *France* and *Holland* with foldiers, or ftocked the wide kingdom of *Poland* with pedlars. Befides fuch of thefe people as anfwer their ends, and having been fo happy

after

after that to survive, generally return hither, which from other countries they seldom did or could, and therefore no just or well grounded fear of depopulation from this cause can possibly arise.

In the next place, this mode of visiting our most distant territories, is so far from thinning the mother country of inhabitants, that it is one, and indeed the principal means of making us populous, by providing such a vast variety of methods for the commodious subsistence by labour and industry, in this country; as before we had these plantations were utterly unknown, and which are also continually increasing, as the commerce with our colonies is increased. Upon this very principle, it may be truly affirmed, that as the plantations preserve the skill and labour of those who go thither, from being lost to their country, as they would be if they went any where else, so by furnishing a great variety of new employments, and different means of subsistence, they take away much of the necessity, and many of those temptations to going abroad, that there were, and which, as has been observed, actually operated to this purpose in former times; and for the same reason that *London* is always full of people, and *Holland* is better inhabited than other countries, that is, because there are more means of living in this city than in other parts of *Britain*, and in that province than through the rest of *Europe*; therefore the support given by the commerce of the colonies, keeps more people in, and attracts more people to *Britain* than otherwise we should have, or indeed without those helps could be able to maintain.

For in the third place, if industry be, as undoubtedly it is, the wealth of a nation, then whatever promotes and rewards industry, is a real accession of wealth. We are but too apt to fancy that the nation can only gain by its foreign commerce and a balance of trade arising from thence; whereas nothing is more certain, than whatever enables men to support themselves in ease and independence, and repays their honest endeavours with a comfortable subsistence, is to *them*, as well as to their country, RICHES; whether it comes to them from abroad, or they acquire it at home. This will appear in the strongest light, if we consider the effects of the sugar trade with respect to *Britain* and to *France*. We formerly, that is in the reign of *Charles the second*, consumed about a thousand hogsheads of sugar, and exported above twice that quantity; at the close of the last century we consumed about twenty thousand hogsheads, and exported about as much. We now consume about fourscore thousand hogsheads, and except in time of war export but very little. On the other hand, the *French* make a great deal of sugar, their consumption is small, and of course they export a great deal in time of peace. But does it follow, because we consume fourscore thousand hogsheads

hogsheads of sugar, and consequently import somewhat more, we gain so much less by it now than when we imported but half the quantity? No certainly, we pay for the sugar now as we did then, that is, we pay for it in our commodities, manufactures, and in all the other ways before described; and therefore it is twice as beneficial to us now as it was then; and if we consume it, this is owing to the increase of our industry, that is of our affluence. If the wealth of *France* was as great, or as generally diffused, that is, if the mass of their people were as thoroughly employed, and thereby as easy in their circumstances, as the bulk of the *British* nation actually are, they would then of course consume much more and export far less.

At the time that great master in commercial science, Sir *Josiah Child*, wrote his excellent treatise, which is now near a century ago, he used many of these arguments in favour of our *sugar* colonies, and treated this subject as amply, and as ably, as could be expected from a person of strong parts, extensive knowledge, and sound judgment. Yet with all these advantages, his writings met with many opponents, and some of them were shrewd people, perfectly skilled in all the arts of managing political controversy, by insisting on popular topics, dressing them out plausibly, and attributing every real and every supposed declension of several branches of our commerce, solely to the

the loss of those who went to the plantations. These they alledge robbed us of our people, and as numbers of men were the wealth as well as strength of a nation, in proportion as these plantations throve, they would continue to draw away more and more, and go on swelling and increasing, while the mother country was gradually wasting in power, and decaying in substance. Sir *Josiah* answered all these dismal apprehensions rationally and solidly; he foresaw and he foretold very different consequences, and yet only the most judicious saw the force of his reasonings, and acquiesced from thence in his opinion.

But we, together with his arguments, which being founded in truth can never lose their weight, have ONE which he could not have, and which is more conclusive than them all, that is EXPERIENCE. The evidence of facts, that evidence which cannot lie, and that evidence therefore which never will deceive, has decided in favour of his reasons, by verifying his predictions. He from his consummate abilities, and his perfect acquaintance with the nature and effects of trade, could even at the distance of a century discern the happy consequences that would in succeeding times attend our settlements. But we, having the benefit of his conceptions, and having also seen those consequences, cannot fail of being convinced of the certainty and the efficacy of their causes. If therefore we presume to look still a little farther, and assert

more

more positively what the same causes may hereafter produce, let not this expose us to censure. For we must be *dwarfs* indeed in understanding, if being thus mounted on this *giant*'s shoulders, and being furnished with so much stronger and steadier lights than he had to use, our prospect should not be somewhat extended, and objects become proportionably more clear.

It is from these principles we have ventured to affirm, not that the inhabitants of *Great Britain* are grown richer, by the mere consuming of fourscore thousand hogsheads of sugar instead of one thousand; but that this increase of our consumption is an indubitable proof of the increase of our riches, consequently of our commerce, and considering how very great a share of this arises from our colonies, this affords the most convincing and conclusive demonstration of the benefits that we have derived from them, as also the clearest evidence that can be desired, of our having in them the most solid resources for the maintenance and extention of our trade, and of course the preservation and augmentation of all those innumerable advantages that apparently attend it. It likewise shews, that notwithstanding *France* in time of peace exports such great quantities of sugar, yet as this visibly arises from the smalness of her home consumption, it must be considered as an incontestible evidence, she has not as a nation drawn the same advantages from her commerce as we have, but is now in that very state we once

D were

were, when though we brought fmaller quantities of fugar from our colonies than we now do, we neverthelefs exported to foreign countries much greater quantities of that commodity than at prefent.

But we would willingly confume what we do, and export alfo; and in procefs of time, without all doubt, we may be able to do this, in confequence of that great acceffion of fugar lands, which we have acquired by the PEACE. But before we can fhew how this may and will be done, it is neceffary to difcufs the fecond previous point in regard to the *neutral* iflands, to fhew how they came to be confidered in that light, and what advantages we are like to derive from their ceafing to be fo confidered, and by their becoming henceforward a part of the territories of *Great Britain*, which we will next endeavour to ftate as plainly and as briefly as it is poffible.

We have before obferved, that the *Englifh* came earlier into the *Weft Indies* than the *French*, which is however a fact the *French* writers as pofitively deny, and found that denial, upon both nations having fixed their firft eftablifhment on the ifland of *St. Chriftophers* on the very fame day. This if it fhould be allowed, as to that ifland, has certainly nothing to do with the reft, and even in regard to this it is admitted by their own writers, that there were fome few perfons of both nations found in that ifland, living in a friendly manner with the *Caribbee Indians* when

this

this supposed discovery was made, so that these ships were not the first of either nation which had been in those parts, and therefore even according to this account, we must look higher for the first adventurers.

The real truth is, that from the reign of queen *Elizabeth*, down to that of *Charles* I. several persons of great rank in *England* had embarked in such discoveries; amongst these may be reckoned the earls of *Nottingham*, *Essex*, *Cumberland*, *Lindsey*, *Pembroke*, Lord *Delawar*, Lord *Thomas Howard*, Lord *Baltimore*, Sir *Walter Ralegh*, Sir *Robert Dudley* (stiled in *Italy* Duke of *Northumberland*) Sir *Richard Greenvile*, Sir *Thomas Gates*, Sir *George Summers*, Sir *Olyff Leigh*, Sir *Thomas Rowe*, Mr. *G. Percy* brother to the Earl of *Northumberland*, Captain *Roger North* brother to Lord *North*, Captain *Charles Parker* brother to Lord *Morley*, Captain *Harcourt*, and others, who most of them exposed their persons, and all employed their purses, in what were then stiled sea-adventures.

As to the settlements in *Virginia*, *New England*, and other parts of *North America*, and the *Bermudas* islands, in the authentic lists of those who contributed to them, may be found the names of the greatest part of the nobility and gentry in the kingdom. But with respect to those who supported the many expeditions for establishing a colony in *Guiana*, which is that upon the river *Surinam*, ceded as has been before mentioned, to the *Dutch*, we are less accurately

curately informed. It was however, in consequence of our several voyages thither, that we became acquainted with, and formed a design of settling some of the islands in the *West Indies*, which according to the best lights that are now in our reach, fell out in this manner.

In the number of those gentlemen who accompanied Captain *Roger North* to *Guiana*, was Mr. *Thomas Warner*, who making an intimate acquaintance there with Captain *Thomas Painton*, a very experienced seaman, he suggested to him how much easier it would be to fix and preserve in good order, a colony in one of the small isles in the *West Indies*, despised and deserted by the *Spaniards*, than in that wide country on the continent, where, for want of sufficient authority, all things were fallen into confusion; and particularly pointed out the island of *St. Christophers*, with which he was so well acquainted, as to mention many good reasons in support of his recommendation. This gentleman dying, Mr. *Warner* returned to *England* in 1620, fully resolved to put his friend's project into execution. He accordingly associated himself with fourteen other persons, (all whose names if necessary might be given) whose circumstances inclined them to concur in his design, and with them he took his passage on board a ship bound for *Virginia*. From thence he and his companions sailed for *St. Christophers*, where they arrived in *January* 1623, and by the month of *September* following, had raised a good crop of tobacco,

(which

(which was to be their staple commodity) but this was totally destroyed by a hurricane. Thus we see how, when, and by whom *St. Christophers* was settled, and this from the relation of the parties themselves.

The new settlement being in this situation, Captain *Jefferson* arrived in the *Hopewell* from *London*, 18th *March* 1624, and it was about this time that the *French* landed, and began to plant on the other side of the island. The *English* colony had the good fortune to preserve their next crop, and with this Captain *Warner* having laden his ship, sailed in *September* 1625 for *London*. It is highly probable, that the *Hopewell* before-mentioned (as we find the same vessel employed thither the next year in that nobleman's service) was actually sent thither at the expence of the Earl of *Carlisle*, who in virtue of that expedition, solicited and obtained in the first year of king *Charles* the first, a warrant for a grant by letters patent under the broad seal of *England*, of the *Caribbee* islands, including also *Barbadoes*. But when that grant came to be actually passed, it was opposed by the earl of *Marlborough*, who being then only Lord *Ley*, but advanced to the rank of Lord High Treasurer of *England*, had obtained in the preceding reign, a grant of the island of *Barbadoes*, and upon full proof of this, and of his having been at great charges in sending ships, men, and stores for settling that island, the Earl of *Carlisle*, in order to carry his point, came to an amicable

micable agreement with the Earl of *Marlborough*, by which he undertook to pay him and his heirs a perpetual annuity of three hundred pounds *per annum*, as a confideration for waving his claim, and then the Earl of *Carlifle*'s patent paffed in 1627. This is as full proof as can be defired, that *Barbadoes* was actually fettled in the reign of *James* the firft, and is founded upon far better authority than that of voyage writers or general hiftorians. For this affair being again canvaffed in council, immediately after the reftoration of King *Charles* II, thefe letters patent were actually produced, and thefe facts before ftated were all clearly proved, as we are fully and authentically informed by the great Earl of *Clarendon*, who as Lord High Chancellor and as a minifter of ftate had very attentively confidered this whole matter.

As truth is always confiftent, fo by comparing the *French* account, and its confequences, with that which we have juft before given, the reality and credibility of the latter will be fully eftablifhed. The *French* tell us, that the Sieur *D'Efnambuc* landed on one fide of the ifland of *St. Chriftophers* on the fame day that Captain *Warner*, afterwards Sir *Thomas Warner* landed on the other fide of the fame ifland: but on what day this was, we are not told, the year however was 1625. Thefe two gentlemen, who had been both attacked in their paffage by the *Spaniards*, entered into an amicable agreement, to fettle and poffefs the country, and mutually

1

mutually to assist each other against the common enemy. They likewise agreed, that each of them should return to his own country, in order to obtain a supply and support. Accordingly the Sieur *D'Esnambuc* with this intention returned to *France*, and having made a very advantageous report of the island which he proposed to settle, a certain number of persons associated as a company for that purpose, under the auspice of the great cardinal *de Richlieu*, who when the Sieur *D'Esnambuc* was ready to sail again to his new colony, thought proper to grant him a commission, the beginning of which, literally translated, runs thus.

" Armand John du Plessis de Richlieu,
" cardinal, counsellor of the king in his coun-
" cils; chief, grand master, and sur-intendant
" of the commerce of *France*, To all to whom
" these presents shall come greeting: maketh
" known, that the Sieur *D'Esnambuc*, and *du*
" *Rossey*, captains belonging to the western de-
" partment of the marine, having given us to
" understand, that they have within these fif-
" teen years past, by licence from the king, and
" the said admiral of *France*, been at great ex-
" pences in the equipping and arming ships and
" vessels, for the searching out of fertile lands
" in a good climate, capable of being possessed
" by the *French*, and therein had used such di-
" ligence as that some time since they had dis-
" covered the islands of *St. Christophers* and
" *Barbadoes*, the one of thirty-five, the other

" of forty-five leagues in circumference, and o-
" ther neighbouring iſlands, all ſituated at the
" entry of *Peru*, from the eleventh to the eigh-
" teenth degree north from the equinoctial line,
" making part of the *Weſt Indies*, which are
" not poſſeſſed by any king or chriſtian prince,
" &c." This commiſſion is dated *October*
" 31ſt, 1626.

On the return of Captain *Warner*, the Earl of *Carliſle* very probably obtained his patent, the preamble of which runs in theſe words. " Whereas our well-beloved and faithful couſin
" and councellor, *James* Lord *Hay*, Baron of
" *Sawley*, Viſcount *Don.uſter*, and Earl of *Car-*
" *liſle*, having a laudable and zealous care to
" increaſe chriſtian religion, and to enlarge the
" territories of our empire, in certain lands ſi-
" tuated to the northward region of the world,
" which region o. iſlands are hereafter deſcri-
" bed, which before were unknown, a by
" certain barbarous men, having no knowledge
" of the divine power, in ſome part poſſeſſed,
" commonly called *Caribbee* iſlands containing
" in them, theſe iſlands following, *viz. St.*
" *Chriſtophers, Granada, St. Vincent, St. Lucia,*
" *Barbadoes, Mittalanea,* (that is what the
" *French* call *Martinique*) *Dominico, Mariga-*
" *lante, Deſſuda, Todos' antes, Guardelupe, An-*
" *tego, Montſerrat, Redendo, Barbudo, Mevis,*
" (properly *Nevis,* by the *French Nieves*) *St.*
" *Bartholomew, St. Martin, Anguilla, Sembrera,*
" and *Enegada*, and other iſlands before found
                                                " out,

" to his great coſt and charges, and brought
" to that paſs, to be a large and copious co-
" lony of *Engliſh*."

There need no greater lights, than common ſenſe and a very general knowledge of the ſubject, to convince any candid peruſer of theſe inſtruments, that the *Engliſh* had been longer in, and were much better acquainted with the *Weſt Indies* than the *French*; ſince the former is ſo poor and vague a deſcription, that it is ſelf-evident they knew not on which ſide of *America* theſe iſlands lay, were acquainted only with *St. Chriſtophers*, and had barely heard of *Barbadoes*, very probably from Captain *Warner*; whereas the latter is a pretty full deſcription of the *Caribbee* iſlands, and ſuch a one as could never have been given, but by perſons who were well acquainted with them, and who very probably had viſited moſt of them. It is for this purpoſe only that we have cited them, and ſhall now proceed in a curſory manner, to ſhew in what manner theſe iſlands have been ſettled by both nations, that the reader may be truly apprized as to the real cauſes of the diſputes that may have ariſen about them.

The iſland of *St. Chriſtopher*, as we have ſeen, was ſettled by both nations in 1625, and in 1627 the two governors, Captain *Warner* and the Sieur *D'Eſnambuc*, made a treaty of partition, by which the *Engliſh* were ſettled on the ſouth and north ſides of the iſland, and the *French* on the eaſt and weſt. In 1629 Don *Frederic de To-*
*le-*

*ledo* came with a great *Spanish* fleet, drove the *French* entirely out of the island, and ruined most of the *English* settlements. However, after he retired, both nations returned to their former quarters, and the island, notwithstanding this and other accidents, was soon very compleatly settled in their respective districts by both *English* and *French*. Under the protectorate, the *French*, as themselves inform us, permitted general *Penn* (or rather some of his squadron) to land their forces, and to march through their territory, in order to oblige the *English* inhabitants to submit themselves to *Cromwell*'s government, which they accordingly did. In the first *Dutch* war in the reign of *Charles* the second, *Lewis* the fourteenth declaring for the States, the *French* in *St. Christophers* dispossessed the *English* of their quarters in the island; who however were restored by virtue of the seventh, eighth, and ninth articles of the treaty of *Breda*, signed *July* the twenty-first, 1667. Immediately after the revolution, the *French* in *St. Christophers* attacked the *English* before there was any declaration of war; and this most flagrant breach of treaty is assigned as one of the causes in the declaration of King *William* and Queen *Mary* against the crown of *France*. However in consequence of this unexpected attack, the *French* expelled the *English* a second time in 1689, but in 1690 General *Codrington* recovered that island, and in their turn drove the *French* intirely out. But they were again restored, in virtue of the

peace

peace concluded at *Ryfwic*, *September* 10th, 1697. In the war relating to the fucceffion of the crown of *Spain*, the *French* were in the very beginning, driven by the *English* out of this ifle, and finally difpoffeffed of their fettlements in *St. Chriftophers*, which were ceded to *Great Britain* by the Treaty of *Utrecht*.

It has been remarked, that the procuring the ceffion of the quarters held by the *French* in this ifland, was objected as a crime to the minifters who negotiated the treaty of *Utrecht*, but poffibly there was more of party in this objection than of public fpirit. The reafon affigned in fupport of it was, that we thereby enabled the *French*, as a nation, to do what otherwife they could not have done for themfelves, that is, to transfer a multitude of able and experienced planters to their larger ifland of *St. Domingo*. But to decide impartially we fhould afk, was this done by the peace or by the war? The *French* had been expelled from *St. Chriftophers* ten years before the peace was made, and had been from that time actually fettled in *St. Domingo*, fo that poffibly it would have been thought as great a hardfhip to have forced them from their new fettlement, as they muft have originally efteemed it to have been driven from their old one. Befides, the multitude was not great, the whole colony confifted but of two thoufand Whites and twelve thoufand flaves. Now it is certain feveral of the beft families remained, and moft of the flaves, which was fo much clear gain

gain to *Britain*. The governors of the *Leeward Islands* made temporary grants of these lands to *British* subjects, who held them under these precarious tenures for many years. Then the *South Sea* company were desirous of obtaining them, but upon the representation of those who had settled and cultivated them, this project was defeated, and at length these lands were sold for the benefit of the public. But to what amount it is not easy to know, this only is certain, that as they contained ten thousand acres of good land, and five thousand acres of an inferior sort, they must have been sold at a pretty round rate; since the late princess of *Orange*'s marriage portion of eighty thousand pounds, was paid out of part of their produce. Upon the whole, it might be very easily proved, that in the space of about sixty years, which have now elapsed since we were in possession of those lands, the sum of upwards of three millions has accrued from them to this nation.

Within five years after we were settled in *St. Christophers*, some of the planters there received such favourable impressions of a small island lying about thirty leagues to the north east, stiled by us *Barbuda*, by the *French*, *Barboude*, and wrote home so favourable an account of it, that one Mr. *Littleton* applied to and obtained a grant from the earl of *Carlisle*, of that little isle to which these new proprietors gave the name of *Dulcina*, and thither they actually removed in 1628. But upon a more accurate survey, they

they became less in love with their new country. They found it indeed healthy and pleasant, but not capable of supplying any staple commodity, and even if that difficulty could have been overcome, without any commodious bay or harbour, and withal liable to frequent invasions from the *Caribbee Indians*, which induced them to desist as speedily from their project of planting it, as they had been hasty in forming it. But notwithstanding this, and that our people in attempting to settle it, have been frequently disturbed by the *Indians*, it was at length peopled and improved, in virtue of a patent granted to an ancestor of the present Sir *William Codrington*, to whom it belonged. The sole produce however of *Barbuda* consists in corn, cattle, and fruits, which did not exempt it from being plundered by the *French*, in the beginning of Queen *Anne*'s war, rather out of spleen to General *Codrington*, who had driven them out of *St. Christophers*, and whom they hoped to have surprised there, than from any profit they proposed to themselves. It recovered however in a short time, and still remains the property of the *Codrington* family.

The same adventurers who quitted *Barbuda*, fixed the same year at *Nevis*, corruptly *Mevis*, by the *French Nieves*, which lies at a very small distance south from *St. Christophers*, and is about twenty-four *English* miles in compass, and in a short time augmented their numbers to one hundred and fifty; for the spirit of planting was

very

very strong in those days. They went on with great success, and were so fortunate in their governors, the greatest blessing can attend a colony, that in the space of a few years, the settlement grew numerous and opulent. At the close of the first *Dutch* war, this island was threatened with an invasion by the joint fleets of *France* and *Holland*, but the inhabitants were seasonably relieved by an *English* fleet, which after a warm and obstinate engagement, forced the enemy to retire with loss. After this, they enjoyed an undisturbed tranquility for near twenty years, and were in so prosperous a condition, that under the government of Sir *William Stapleton*, they mustered three thousand effective men in this small island, though their whole force thirty years ago, did not amount to so many hundred. In the war with *France* in the reign of King *William*, they were not attacked, but on the contrary acted offensively, and did the enemy much mischief. In Queen *Anne*'s war they were less fortunate, for the *French* landing here on *Good-Friday*, 1706, they were compelled by a superior force, and by their being abandoned by most of the *Negroes*, to submit to a capitulation, which was signed on *Easter Day*, and which was very ill observed in respect to them; and in regard to their slaves, who by their desertion ruined their masters, and for this were promised good terms: the enemy, contrary to the agreement with them, clapped numbers on board their ships, and sold them to the *Spaniards* to work in their mines. By this heavy calamity and subsequent depredations, the colony was brought very low; but having been effectually protected ever since, is through the spirit and industry of the inhabitants put again into a very flourishing condition.

In the year 1632, Sir *Thomas Warner* sent a small number of his people from *St. Christophers* to *Montserrat*, lying to the south-east, being of a round figure, a little mountainous island, which owes its healthiness and security to that circumstance. It was become a very populous and well-improved settlement, when attacked and reduced by the *French* in the beginning of the reign of King *Charles* the second. But being restored to its master by the twelfth article of the treaty of *Breda*, it very speedily recovered its former splendor. When the next war broke out with *France*; soon after the revolution the people of *Montserrat* acted with great vigour and spirit, by which they kept their enemies at a distance. But by these extraordinary though honourable efforts, their numbers were considerably diminished. This exposed them in the reign of Queen *Anne* to be extremely harrassed by the *French*; and even after the cessation of arms was concluded, Mr. *Cossard* landed here, and in a great measure ruined the island. For this, it was stipulated in the eleventh article of the treaty of *Utrecht*, that an enquiry should be made into the damages which the people of *Montserrat* had suffered. But it does not appear,

pear that any such enquiry was ever made, or that the least compensation was received.

At what time *Antego*, which is the largest of our *Leeward Islands*, lying about twenty leagues east from *St. Christophers*, near ten leagues north-east from *Montserrat*, upwards of fifty miles in circumference, was first settled, does not appear: but it is pretty certain, that during the government of Sir *Thomas Warner* in *St. Christophers*, some *English* families removed hither. The prevailing opinion that it was entirely destitute of fresh water, hindered any great resort of inhabitants, and it certainly made no great figure until granted by King *Charles* the second to the Lord *Willoughby* of *Parham*, about three years after the restoration, who sent his brother thither to promote the settlement. This gentleman, finding some *French* who had retired thither, and lived very amicably with the *English* then there, treated them a little harshly, which induced them to quit the island, and upon the breaking out of the war in 1666, they gave their countrymen such informations, as to the weakness of the colony, and the properest means of attacking it, that they undertook to reduce it, and carried their point. It was however restored, as well as *Montserrat*, by the 12th article of the treaty of *Breda*, as by the 10th article of the same treaty the country of *Acadie* or *Nova Scotia* was restored to the *French*. Upon the return of peace, the colony began once more to flourish, and made some considerable progress in the space of twenty years. Its greatest improvements however, were owing to the singular skill and activity of Colonel *Codrington*, who removed thither from *Barbadoes*, and who by his perfect knowledge in planting, and by his obliging communications, quickly gave a new face to affairs, and rectified many mistakes that had been of an old standing, so that the sugars here came to bear as good a price, as in the other islands, which they had not done before. In the war that followed the revolution, the people of this island acted vigorously under the command of General *Codrington* against the *French*, in attacking and plundering the islands of *Marigalante*, *St. Bartholomew* and *St. Martin*'s; and if we except some trifling depredations committed upon the coast by *French* privateers, suffered little or nothing. They were no less active in that of Queen *Anne*, when General *Codrington* made an attempt upon *Guadaloupe* with great appearance of success, and in all probability would have conquered that island, if it had not been for an unhappy difference with the officer who commanded the naval force. In this reign, the seat of government, with respect to the *Leeward Islands*, was transferred to *Antego*, where it has ever since remained. This no doubt has contributed not a little to that prosperous and flourishing condition in which it now is, together also with another circumstance, *viz.* the conveniency of that which is called *English* Harbour, for the careen-

E          ing

ing ships of war, when that is requisite in this part of the world, and which harbour is at this time improving in such a manner, as that it may be able to receive ships of as large size as are ever sent hither.

These that have been mentioned, are those that pass generally under the name of the *British Leeward Islands*; but besides these we have been at different times possessed of several others in these parts. In 1666 we dispossessed the *Dutch* of *St. Eustatia*, lying a little to the north-west of *St. Christophers*, which however was recovered the next year, by the joint forces of the *Dutch* and *French*. In the war after the revolution, that island being taken from the *Dutch* by the *French*, the latter were dispossessed of it by Sir *Timothy Thornhill*, who left a small corps therein of *English* troops, to protect the inhabitants, 'till it was finally restored to the *Dutch* by the treaty of *Ryswic*, who have enjoyed it peaceably ever since.

The island of *Santa Cruz*, or as the *French* call it, *Sainte Croix*, was visited by the *English* in 1587, and about 1635 it was settled by the *English* and *Dutch* in the same manner that *St. Christophers* had been by the *English* and *French*. In 1645, the *Dutch* governor killed the *English* governor in his house, upon which a civil war began in the island, in which the *Dutch* governor was killed. At length a pacification ensued, and the *Dutch* chose a new governor, who is said to have been invited by the *English* governor to his house, and there slain. After which, the *Dutch* were driven entirely out of the island, and there being amongst them about one hundred and twenty *French*, they at their own request were sent to *Guadaloupe*. The *Spaniards* knowing that the *English*, though now sole masters of the island, could be but weak, after all these intestine troubles, attacked them in 1650, and extirpated all that they found there. The *Dutch* then made a bold effort to recover it, and were in like manner destroyed by the superior force of the *Spaniards*. The *French* from *St. Christophers* next attempted to expel the *Spaniards*, which though not without some difficulty they accomplished, and held it peaceably till about the year 1695 or 1696, when they thought fit to withdraw their colony, and it has been since occupied by the *Danes*, to whom, according to an opinion that universally prevails in the *West-Indies*, it was sold by the *French* for a very large sum of money. But though possessed by the *Danes*, it is at present chiefly inhabited, as we before observed, by *British* subjects, who have settled it under their protection.

We hold besides these, the island of *Anguilla*, so called from its form, which resembles that of a *snake*, lying twenty-six leagues north-east from *St. Cruz*, and near fifteen north from *St. Christophers*, the islands of *St. Bartholomew* and *St. Martin* lying between them; and though it be but small yet it is pleasant, fertile, and by no means contemptible in its value. Amongst those islands that are stiled the *Virgins*, or *las Virgines*,

*Virgines,* which were so called by the *Spaniards,* we hold *Tortola,* a very fine island, as large and as valuable as *Montserrat,* which was taken from the *Dutch* in the first war against them, in the reign of King *Charles* the second. *Spanish Town* (or rather *Peniston*) by the *Spaniards Virgin Gorda,* or the *Great Virgin,* which though of no great extent, yields commodities to a considerable value. Besides these, there are a great many small islands and islets, such as *Great Dog, Little Dog, Scrub, Great Cumanus, Little Cumanus, Guiana, Beef Island, Jerusalem, Round Rock, Coopers Isle, Salt Island,* &c. from which the sea is thought to be continually, though slowly, subsiding, and of course the land gradually increasing. In the bosom of these *Virgins,* if that expression may be excused, there is the finest bason of water that can be conceived, land-locked from all winds by the regular disposition of these isles, most of which are cultivated, and yield no small quantities of cotton and provisions, from which some thousand of Whites derive tolerable estates, and many thousand *Negro* slaves a comfortable subsistence; there being none of our settlements in which they live more at their ease or in greater plenty. We likewise twice settled, and were twice exterminated by the *Spaniards* from an island more valuable than any of these, called by the natives *Boriquen,* by which name also *Puerto Rico* was known, to which it is very near, but from the multitude of those animals, that are found upon it, called

by

by our seamen *Crab Island*. We will now turn our eyes more particularly to the acquisitions of the *French*.

As soon as their establishment in *St. Christophers* began to thrive, Mr. *Desnambuc* their governor, formed projects for further acquisitions, and of these he wrote his sentiments to the company in *France*, where they met with such approbation, that in the year 1635 they fitted out Messieurs *du Plessis* and *l'Olive*, with instructions to settle a colony in any of the three islands they should judge most convenient, which had been mentioned to them by the governor of *St. Christophers*. They sailed accordingly from *Dieppe*, and landed first on *Martinico*, but disliking the mountainous appearance of that country, they proceeded next to *Guadaloupe*, on which they landed, and took possession *June* the 8th, 1635.

To speak with propriety, this *French* colony is established on two islands, the one properly called *Guadaloupe*, which is upwards of one hundred *English* miles in circumference, the other *Grand Terre*, which is above one hundred and sixty in circuit, divided by a narrow arm of the sea, which is called the *Salt River*. *Guadaloupe* proper is certainly a very fine island, and so much of it as can be cultivated, is very rich and fertile, but then the mountains in the middle of the island occupy near the one half, and the rivers and rivulets which descend from them on both sides, so as constantly and plentifully to water the flat country, are the great sources both of pleasure and profit. On the other hand, *Grand Terre* which, as we have already observed, is the larger island of the two, is all flat ground, and of consequence has no rivers, indeed scarce any water at all, except what is saved in cisterns, which renders it unhealthy in respect to the inhabitants, and subjects them frequently to short crops, from their canes being burned up, and even when there are greater quantities of sugar than in *Guadaloupe*, that sugar is not equally valuable.

As to the produce of this island, we have had such a variety, and those too such different accounts, that it is very difficult to state any thing with certainty, or at least that will be thought so by the generality of readers. Mr. *Savary*, in a work of his addressed to that great minister Mr. *Colbert*, in the year 1679, tells us it produced then four thousand three hundred seventy-five *French* hogsheads of sugar, of eight hundred weight each. In the *Dictionnaire de Commerce*, published by the descendants of that gentleman and their associates in 1742, it was said to produce five thousand such hogsheads, which agrees very well with the exports in the year 1759, which was the first after it was reduced by the *British* arms, when we imported 3625 such hogsheads, tho' very possibly this might not be its entire produce, but that a part might find its way into *Europe* from *St. Eustatia*. In the next year, twenty-one thousand and sixteen hogsheads, and in the succeeding, which was the year 1761, twenty-

twenty-five thousand five hundred and eighteen, whence not without great probability, it has been surmised, that part of the produce of *Martinico* passed through *Guadaloupe*, and under the name of her sugars into *England*.

The island of *Martinico* received that name from the *Spaniards*, and is called by the *French Martinique*. The *Indian* name was *Medanina* or *Metanino*, but in *de Laet*'s maps, and in all our old authors, we find it called *Mittalanea*. It is certainly a very fine and spacious isle, about one hundred and eighty miles in circumference, but very irregular in its form. The air is but indifferent, it is very mountainous, and many of those mountains are rocky and inaccessible, others as far as they are cultivable, fertile and pleasant. There are about forty rivers, and rivulets, which water this country, and some of the former overflow in such a manner as to produce great inconveniences. Besides, from this humidity joined to the extreme heat of the climate, it is very much infested with venomous creatures, as well as some very noxious and troublesome insects.

It was settled by Mr. *Desnambuc*, who having intelligence that Messrs. *Du Plessis* and *L'Olive* were commissioned to make new establishments, he thought it expedient to try how far his projects were capable of being executed by himself, and the forces he could raise in his own government of *St. Christophers*. Sailing accordingly from thence, he debarked with about a hundred men,

men, *July* the fixth, 1635, in this ifland, which was then well inhabited by the *Caribbee Indians*, with whom he endeavoured to maintain a fair correfpondence, and recommended this to Mr. *du Pont*, whom he left there as his lieutenant. Things remained for many years in this fituation, till upon fome offence taken, the *Indians*, through thofe mountainous tracks that were thought altogether impaffable, broke in upon the *French* colony, and were not without great difficu'ty repulfed, and at length about the year 1658, forced to abandon the ifland, and retire to *Dominica* and *St. Vincent*. After their expulfion, that part of the ifle which they inhabited, was divided by the conquerors and very quickly fettled. *Martinico* was for a long feries of time the principal refort of the *Buccaneers*, or, as the *French* ftile them, *Flibufteirs*, who from thence in the firft *Dutch* war incommoded our fettlements extremely. In the fecond *Dutch* war it was attacked by Admiral *de Ruyter* in 1674, who did there a great deal of mifchief. In King *William*'s war it felt more feverely the weight of our power. It efcaped better in the war of Queen *Anne*, and at the opening of the laft war was thought to be fo well fortified, and to have fuch a ftrength within itfelf, as that it had nothing to fear; and perhaps this notion received fome countenance from the failing of our firft attempt, but it was afterwards forced as well as *Guadaloupe* had been before, to fubmit to his majefty's triumphant arms.

As *Martinico* is the seat of the *French* government, in respect to her islands, and in consequence of that being the residence of her governor-general, it has always made a greater figure than any of the rest. There are upon it four considerable fortifications, the town of *St. Pierre* is larger and better built than any in her other islands, and the commerce here in time of peace proportionably greater. The products of this island are sugar, coffee, cocoa, cotton, indigo, ginger, pimento, drugs, dying woods, and some more inconsiderable articles. In 1679 it produced six thousand two hundred and fifty *French* hogsheads of sugar, in 1742 its produce was computed at seven thousand five hundred hogsheads, and it has since raised twenty-five thousand, but a great part of these were refined sugars, and of consequence the more valuable. If we may credit one of the latest performances that has been published in *France*, the shipping employed from that kingdom to this island, consisted in three hundred vessels of between one hundred and two hundred and fifty tons.

In 1635 they made an attempt upon the island of *Statia*, or as the *French* call it *Saint Eustache*, but without success. They were however more fortunate in the second *Dutch* war, and also in that of the reign of King *William*, but they were obliged to quit it, and the future possession of it was secured to the *Dutch* by the treaty of *Ryswic*. In 1638 they endeavoured to fix themselves in the island of *St. Martin*, which

though

though small in itself, is a fertile and pleasant island, but chiefly valuable on account of its salt ponds, which induced the *Spaniards* to build a fort and to maintain a garrison therein for its defence. It was this likewise that engaged them to dispossess these invaders; but about ten years after they abandoned the island, of which the *Dutch* having notice, they presently debarked a body of men there, but the *French* the same year, that is in 1648, sent a force to recover it. Upon which, to prevent the effusion of blood, it was agreed to divide it between the two nations, in the same manner that *St. Christophers* had been. In this state it has continued ever since. The *French* indeed have more than once endeavoured to withdraw their colony, but the inhabitants, better pleased to remain there, have concluded what they call a concordat with the *Dutch*, by which in time of war each nation is bound reciprocally to assist the other, and under this protection the *French* continued quiet, during the wars in King *William*'s and Queen *Anne*'s reigns, and have not been molested since. The very same year, in which they went first to *St. Martin*'s, they sent a very small strength to attack the island of *Granada*, then possessed by the *Caribbee Indians*, who disputed it with them for many years, as we shall hereafter have occasion to shew in its proper place.

The island of *St. Bartholomew*, or as the *French* call it, *St. Barthelemi*, which lies three leagues from *St. Martin*, and six from *St. Christophers*,

*stophers*, and which is about twenty five miles in compass, was possessed by them in 1648, it is a very pleasant and a very wholesome island, produces all the necessaries of life, together with some cotton, a great deal of good timber, and some drugs, but no commodities of any great value. It has however a very safe and commodious port, where Sir *Timothy Thornhil* landed in 1689, and reduced the island, which the inhabitants were notwithstanding allowed to repossess, and remained quietly under the protection of the crown of *Great Britain*, till it was restored by the peace of *Ryswic*, since which it seems to have continued unmolested. About the same time they settled those three small islands called *the Saints*, upon which the *Spaniards* bestowed the name, because they discovered them on *All Saints* day. They lie between *Guadaloupe* and *Dominica*, two of them only being inhabited, the third, which is a rock, affording by its situation a harbour for the rest. They are tolerably inhabited, though without fresh water, and the people in them subsist by raising provisions, of which in time of war they are liable to be plundered, and they are chiefly remarkable for the shipwreck of *Francis* Lord *Willoughby*, who was lost near them in the first *Dutch* war.

MARIGALANTE derives its name from *Columbus*'s ship. It is nearly round in its form, and about fifty *English* miles in compass, lies four leagues south-east from *Grande Terre*, and

seven-

seventeen north from *Martinique*. The *French* made many attempts to settle it before they succeeded, being more than once cut off by the *Caribbee Indians*, but in 1652 they carried their point, and obliged the natives to retire to *Dominica*, since which time they have been possessed of it. This island is in general flat, very indifferently watered, tolerably well cultivated, though it has been thrice reduced by the *British* arms, exclusive of the last war, when, after the taking of *Guadaloupe* it yielded without resistance. The soil when cultivated, is said to be fertile, and at the time it came into our possession, it produced about a thousand hogsheads of sugar, besides most of the other commodities common throughout the rest of the islands.

D ESEADA, *Dessuda*, or *Desirade*, is a smaller island than the former, lying four leagues east from *Grande Terre*, and between six and seven north-east from *Marigalante*. It has a deep black soil, produces much timber, and particularly lignum vitæ of a large size, some sugar, but a large quantity of cotton, which is esteemed the very best in the *French* isles. There is in it a good harbour for privateers, and it was very well inhabited, when in the last war it shared the same fate with *Guadaloupe* and *Marigalante*, the people esteeming themselves happy, to share also in that most favourable capitulation granted to those islands.

We have now run through all the *French* islands, in respect to their size, situation and produce,

produce, excepting the part that they hold in *St. Domingo* or *Hispaniola*, which being one of the greater *Antilles*, would be more properly opposed to *Jamaica* than to the *Leeward Islands*, and therefore lies without our plan. From this succinct detail, we see in a very narrow compass what is the true extent of the *French* territory, and may from thence collect, what a degree of strength may result from the combined force of their islands, and to what height their navigation and commerce may arise from the cultivation of these countries; for to these they will be hereafter confined, as there seems to be now no opening left for them to augment their dominions at the expence of any other nation in these parts. But in order to understand this subject more clearly, and to acquire a more distinct prospect of what may hereafter happen to both nations, a few general observations will be necessary, founded in the relation between causes and effects, deduced chiefly from what has happened to them in former times.

At their first settlement in the *West Indies*, the *English* were more wisely directed and better supported as the *French* writers themselves confess, and indeed it is to them we owe all our information, than their colony, though planted under the powerful protection of Cardinal *Richlieu*. It was this that enabled us to spread ourselves so soon into different islands, and it appears that our countrymen chose the nearest, though small and not over fertile, that they

they might be the better able to assist each other, and that all their settlements in those small islands lying near the sea, their cultivation and their commerce, might from thence derive reciprocal advantages. In this they followed the true spirit and genius of planting, by which, in the space of a very few years, they became numerous, brought their lands into good order, and drove for those times, and that commodity in which they chiefly dealt, which was *Tobacco*, a very regular and lucrative trade, to which they bent all their endeavours, and from which they derived a prosperous security.

The *French*, on the other hand, were slower and less successful in their improvements, for reasons that will be presently explained; but as soon as they had acquired a little strength, according to the enterprizing temper of the nation, they began to meditate new conquests, and to affect a wide extent of territory, instead of making the most of what they possessed. They were not in those days much inclined to industry, had very imperfect notions of trade, and no constant or regular communication with their mother country. But this did not hinder them from attempting to seize, as we have seen, various islands, and where they wanted force they made use of policy, cajoling the *Indians* while they were superior to them in strength, and as their power increased, picking quarrels with them, and driving them gradually out of their possessions; so that for the space of near thirty

thirty years, their chief employment was war, and their principal aim the acquisition of territory, in which by their discipline and perseverance, they gradually succeeded.

Both the *English* and the *French* began to form their establishments in the *West Indies*, when the affairs of their respective nations were in an unsettled condition at home; so that instead of wondering at any delay in their progress, there is more reason to be surprised that they grew at all instead of not growing faster. In respect to the *English*, the Earl of *Carlisle*, who was really the patron, as well as proprietor of the *Leeward Islands*, died in 1636, and left his affairs in great confusion. The civil war broke out a few years after, during which our colonies were in a manner left to themselves, and their inhabitants were obliged to shift as well as they could. But the *Dutch*, always attentive to their own interest, and in consequence of that attentive to a certain degree to the interests of those by whom their own may be best promoted, fell into a trade with our islands, encouraged them in turning their thoughts to the cultivation of sugar, furnished them with the utensils necessary for their works, and assisted them likewise with *Negroes*. After the ruin of the King's affairs, many who had been officers in his army, took shelter in *Barbadoes* and the other islands, where they became planters, and King *Charles* the second being then in *Holland*, sent *Francis* Lord *Willoughby* of *Parham* from thence, with the title of of governor of *Barbadoes* and the *Leeward Islands*, who was chearfully received and obeyed in that quality by the inhabitants, whom he found in a thriving and prosperous condition.

But in 1651, the parliament sent out Sir *George Ayscue* with a squadron of ships of war, to reduce those islands to their obedience, which though he met with a considerable resistance he effected, seized and confiscated many *Dutch* ships, and put an end to their correspondence with the subjects of that republic. It was in these times of confusion that we were dispossessed of *Santa Cruz*, and our colonies were twice extirpated in *Boriquen* or *Crab Island* by the *Spaniards*, which though scarce mentioned by our historians, were very great national losses, if we may compute the value of those islands according to the profits that have arisen to us from those that are left.

CROMWELL's war with *Spain*, though it procured to us *Jamaica*, weakened our other islands by the numbers drawn out of them for the *St. Domingo* expedition, and then by the supplies sent to people our new conquest. The natural consequence of this was, that as we have already seen, the first *Dutch* war in the reign of King *Charles* the second, which happened but eight years afterwards, and in which we had to contend both with that nation and the *French*, proved so unfortunate to us in *America*, where, as we have already observed, we were forced to redeem our *Islands* from the *French*, at the expence

expence of *Nova Scotia*, and to give up *Surinam*, that we might retain *New York* and its dependencies, which, during our Troubles the *Dutch* had seized, on the continent of *North America*. Both these cessions by the way, plainly prove what the sentiments were, both of *Great-Britain* and of *France*, with respect to the consequence of those countries.

The *French* in this respect, that is, as to national tranquillity, were not at all in a happier situation. The first company, though erected, as we have observed, with the participation, and under the auspice of the great Cardinal *de Richlieu*, had no larger a fund than *forty-five thousand* livres, and that able minister had the mortification to see its affairs in a very declining state before his death, which happened in 1642. After this, their concerns fell into such confusion, and the distraction of the government under the first years of *Mazarine*'s ministry, were so unfavourable for establishments of this nature, that in 1661, the company sold to the Bailiff *de Poinci*, in trust for his order of *Malta*, the islands of *St. Christopher, St. Bartholomew, St. Martin,* and *St. Croix*. In like manner they disposed of *Guadaloupe, Marigalante, Desirade,* and the *Saints*, to the Sieur *Houel*, and *Martinico* and *Granada* to the Sieur *Parquet*, in which sales nothing was reserved to the crown of *France* but the bare title of sovereignty; and having thus parted with their possessions, this first company was dissolved.

F  When

When LEWIS XIV. with the affiftance of abler minifters, came to look into his own affairs, he by letters patent dated in *July* 1664, erected a new *Weſt-India* company, to which were affigned all the poffeffions of *France* in *America*, both continent and iflands, and this company had funds proportioned to the extent of their powers, and to the views of the King and his minifter in erecting it. They were directed in the firſt place, to purchafe from the order of *Malta* and the other proprietors, the iflands which they held; they were next enjoined to refcue the trade of all thefe fettlements out of the hands of the *Dutch*, who had carried it on all this time; and laftly, they were charged with the greateſt part of the expences of the war maintained againſt *England*; and when with much fpirit and at a vaft charge they had anfwered all thefe important purpofes, and that too in fo fhort a fpace as nine years, they were diffolved, becaufe they had anfwered thofe purpofes, and fo were no longer neceffary; and from the time they were fuppreffed in 1674, the crown of *France* entered into the full poffeffion of thefe iflands; the trade of which, as much as poffible, was confined to *France*, but as we fee by the memorials prefented to the *council* of *trade* in 1701, they were fo perplexed and embarraffed by the *Guinea* company, and the intrigues of the farmers general, that all the great views, and all the wife contrivances, of the famous *Colbert* and his fucceffors, were in a great mea-

fure

fute though not wholly defeated. It was to these memorials, penned with equal skill and spirit, that the *French* ministers stood indebted for the true knowledge of the nature of this commerce, the value of their islands, and the many advantageous consequences, that might follow from things being put into a right train.

But it must not be understood, that domestick confusions and intestine troubles, have been fatal only to these two nations, in this part of the globe; the like cause has produced exactly the same effect, with respect to others. It was the falling of *Portugal* under the subjection of *Spain*, that not only gave occasion to the *Dutch* to attack *Brazil*, who had otherwise no cause of quarrel whatever with the *Portuguese*, but also dispirited and discouraged them to such a degree, that a great part of the country was lost; and thus it appears that a very small state, such as *Portugal* was, while well governed under a series of wise and brave princes, was able to make a glorious figure, and to become one of the greatest maritime powers in the world; and yet, when united as a province, to a still greater power, from the discord and discontent which this occasioned, became so weak and so unlike to what it had formerly been, that the people of *Holland*, under a free, mild, and prudent administration, gained such an ascendant, as to erect on the ruins of the *Portuguese* empire in the *East-Indies* and *South America*, an empire of their own.

But when the *Portuguese* recovered their independency, though broken and extenuated by having been under the *Spanish* yoke, they recovered also so much strength and spirit, as to attack their conquerors, and that with so much success, as to oblige them to leave *Brazil*, which however they might not perhaps have atchieved, if the *Dutch* themselves had not been in a great degree disunited, since in all probability, the *States* would never have submitted to evacuate and quit their claim to *Brazil*, if the *Zelanders*, who were the most interested in that valuable acquisition, had not been at that time warmly attached to the Prince of ORANGE, afterwards King *William* III. from whom the *States* were then disposed to wrest the dignities hereditary in his family, and from thence inclined to desert, for the furtherance of their own views, a conquest of such consequence to the republic.

It was likewise to the imbecility of the three last monarchs of the House of *Austria* in *Spain*, that her dominions in *America* suffered as they did. It was this that rendered it practicable for the *English* and *French* with such inconsiderable forces, to possess themselves of the lesser *Antilles*, and the *Dutch* after their example, to fix themselves in those islands which they still continue to possess. It was this, that rendered it practicable for the *Buccaneers*, *Flibustiers*, or *Freebooters*, to harrass, plunder, and ruin, almost all the rich and great places near the sea, in *South* as well as *North America*, unowned and unsup-

unsupported by any other power, though connived at and privately assisted by several. It was this also, that rendered them unable to defend *Jamaica* against us, and put it in the power first of the *Buccaneers*, and then of the *French* to dispossess them of one moiety of the island of *St. Domingo* or *Hispaniola*. In a word, it appears from hence, impossible for a maritime state to maintain her naval power and the territories which in right of that she possesses *abroad*, if consummate wisdom does not direct, and the most perfect harmony sustain her *counsels* at *home*.

We are sometimes apt, from pride and self-conceit, to exaggerate and overvalue the performances of our own nation; and at others, either through envy or caprice, to depreciate them, in comparison of foreigners. But if laying aside this over-weaning passion, and rejecting all unbecoming prejudice, we are content to look for *truth* through the medium of *facts*, we shall be able to discern clearly, that in respect to our *West-India* islands, we in the first place improved much faster than the *French*; for *Barbadoes* was arrived at the very meridian of its glory, precisely at that period, when by disolving their *second West-India* company, the *French* but began to put their islands into a posture of thriving, or at least into a posture of thriving for the benefit of *France*.

In the next place, we have carried our improvements much farther; for all the advantages we have derived from *Barbadoes*, and the reſt of our *Leeward Iſlands*, we have derived from a *fifth*, perhaps the error would not be great if we ſaid, from a ſixth part of the land, that is in the hands of the *French*. This certainly does very great honour to the ſkill and induſtry of the *Britiſh* planters, and it is an honour which ought not to be undervalued, ſince in this kind of national conteſt, it is the greateſt at which a people can poſſibly arrive. It is ſtill of farther conſequence, as it ſerves to lay a rational foundation for our future hopes; ſince if we have by the ſucceſs of our arms, and in virtue of that by the terms of the peace lately concluded, acquired as it will hereafter appear we have, a much larger extent of territory than all we before poſſeſſed, there are good grounds to expect, that our countrymen will be no leſs ſucceſsful in their future labours; and that this may be conſidered, as the epoch, from whence our poſterity may date the increaſe of their proſperity, of which even the preſent generaration may enjoy conſiderable fruits, as well as the comfortable proſpect of ſtill greater profits, that in conſequence of future improvements, will ariſe in time to come.

But this is not all. If our improvements were not only quicker and greater, than thoſe of the *French*; they have been alſo much more conducive to the wealth and power of the mother country; they have augmented our national ſtock; they have extended our navigation;

tion; they have added strength and splendour to our naval force. All this may not only be fairly affirmed, but may also be fully proved. We have seen that in the first *Dutch* war, in the reign of *Charles* II. we were not able to defend these islands, though, considered simply in respect to themselves, they were then at least as strong as they are now. But during the peace that succeeded, the benefits that accrued to this nation from those colonies, had such an influence on the affairs of this country, that in every succeeding war, we have been able to defend them, by a maritime force from hence, and in the last war, not only to defend, but to deprive our enemies of the greatest part of their possessions. This, therefore, is a conclusive argument, in support of the proposition, that we have last advanced, and taking the whole into our consideration, will teach us to think justly and in a becoming manner of the importance of these settlements, and to conceive a true idea of what does so much honour to our national character; the reciprocal advantages that are derived to us from the industry of their inhabitants, and that protection which we have afforded to them, in consequence of those large and long continued streams of wealth, that we have drawn from them.

We may from this historical deduction, clearly discern, that it was upon the first establishment of our colonies, they were so thoroughly inhabited, more especially by whites. We may learn

learn from the letters written by *Cromwell*'s land and sea officers, during their *American* expedition, that our islands then swarmed with people, and that more than one half of that puissant force, the greatest incontestibly that till then, had ever been seen in those parts, was raised in those islands. To descend a little to particulars, *three thousand five hundred* were taken out of *Barbadoes*, and *fifteen hundred* from the other islands, though *Antigua*, the largest of them, was not at that period, in any degree settled. A little after the restoration, that is before the first *Dutch* war, we have the authentic testimony of Mr. *Lewis Roberts*, that there were *forty thousand* whites in the colony of *Surinam*. The *French* writers confirm these accounts, and assert that the *English* were so numerous in their islands, that they were forced to discharge a part of their inhabitants upon the continent. But at this time, surely men did not go there so much from motives of profit, as from the spur of necessity. They went thither, because they knew not where else to go. They went, because they wanted employment, and knew not how to live at home. Persons in this situation, had there been no colonies, would have left this country ; and therefore happy for this country, that they had colonies to which they might go. This is a demonstration drawn from facts, of the truth of those principles, upon which Sir *Josiah Child* reasoned. But does the present state of our colonies shew, that they have been ever since

such

such a drain upon this country? Are there now in all the *Leeward Islands*, as many whites as there were *sixty* years ago in the single island of *Barbadoes*; or go there any number thither even now, but from motives of necessity? If this be the case, as most certainly it is, and if most of those who go there, in narrow circumstances, find their way back, if they survive to see an alteration in their circumstances, does not this fulfil his prophecy, and can we any longer have the least shadow of doubt, as to the certainty of those principles upon which he argued? The colonies, at least the *sugar* colonies, are no more than transmarine provinces of *Great Britain*; the countries they inhabit belong as much to us, as any of our counties; and the people in them are as much our countrymen. It is WE that reap the benefit of their labours, the wealth they acquire centers *here*, and it is that wealth, and the strength arising from it, that enables us to defend THEM, against their enemies and ours. This is the true and real state of the question, which every man enlightened by common sense, and actuated by public spirit, will easily comprehend, and none but people of narrow and contracted minds, will suffer themselves to entertain separate ideas of the ISLAND of GREAT BRITIAN and the EMPIRE of GREAT BRITAIN. No, let politicians and statesmen conceive the bounds of both to be the same, and afford his majesty's subjects the same protection, whether they live within the *verge* of his *royal palace*, or live

live for his and their country's service, on the very *verge* of his extensive dominions.

After the conclusion of the peace of *Breda*, the great value of our colonies appeared; and as all matters relative to commerce, were then frequently canvassed, and of course generally understood, great attention was shewn to them, which of course raised a spirit of emulation in the *French*, and as Mr. *Colbert* had dictated both the establishment of the company in 1664, and the suppression of it nine years after, so the principles, with which he inspired his master, induced *Lewis* XIV. soon after the accession of King *James* II. to propose a treaty for regulating the affairs of both crowns in *America*, so as to prevent all future disputes between their subjects. This after a long negotiation, was actually concluded and signed at *Whitehall*, under the title of a a treaty of peace, good correspondence, and neutrality in *America, November* 5, 1686, by the *French* ambassador Mr. *Barillon,* and by the Lord High Treasurer, Lord High Chancellor, president of the council, and two secretaries of state on the part of *Great Britain*. The points settled by this treaty were; *First*, That the subjects of both crowns, should live in perfect peace and amity with each other, that they might reciprocally pursue their respective improvements, without interruption or apprehension. *Secondly*, Both crowns to retain in their full extent, their possessions, prerogatives, and jurisdictions; by which it appeared they meant to secure the advantages

vantages refulting from thefe colonies, to their refpective dominions; and therefore the fubjects of either crown, were not to enter into the ports, or trade, or in any manner interfere, with the commerce belonging to the fubjects of the other. *Thirdly,* In cafes of neceffity however, the fhips of either power, whether merchant-men or men of war, might enter the ports of the other nation, under certain reftrictions; and in cafe of wrecks, the utmoft care was to be taken on both fides, to leffen the misfortune to the fuffering party. *Fourthly,* It was ftipulated, that the *Englifh* might load falt at the ponds in the ifland of *St. Chriftopher,* and that the *French* might enter the mouths of rivers in the faid ifland, to take frefh water; but in both cafes this was to be done in open day, with a flag flying, and after the thrice firing of a gun. *Fifthly,* The fubjects of either nation, were not to harbour either wild inhabitants, or the flaves or goods, which they might have taken from the fubjects of the other nation. *Sixthly,* It was agreed, that if any depredations were committed by the privateers of either power, full fatisfaction fhould be made for the injury; and that this might be the more eafily done, commanders of privateers were to give fecurities in both countries, in *one thoufand* pounds fterling, then equal to *thirteen thoufand* livres, and that the fhip alfo fhould be liable to make fatisfaction for any act of injuftice, by them committed. *Seventhly,* Neither party were to give countenance or affiftance to pirates

pirates or free-booters, nor in cafe of a war between either of the crowns with any other power, were the fubjects of the other power, to apply for commiffions, or to act under any fuch commiffions, to the prejudice of the other contracting party. *Eighthly*, No differences, difputes, or difturbances arifing in *America*, were to create a rupture in *Europe*, but in cafe they could not be determined in the fpace of a year in that part of the world, they were to be ftated and fent home, by both parties. *Ninthly*, In cafe any war broke out in *Europe*, between the two crowns, a ftrict *neutrality* was to be maintained by their fubjects in *America* notwithftanding.

The ftipulations in this treaty of neutrality, feem to be equally calculated for the common benefit of both nations, but in reality were moft ufeful to the *French*, who at this juncture were but entering into the bufinefs of planting, were fcattered through a number of large iflands, by which they were not only rendered weak, but at the fame time, extremely fenfible of their own weaknefs; which was what chiefly inclined them to this neutrality. On the other hand, our fubjects, in a very profperous and flourifhing condition, were extremely defirous of being free from thofe inconveniences, which the libertine fpirit of the *French Buccaneers*, and *Flibuftiers*, often produced, notwithftanding the two crowns lived in good intelligence with each other in *Europe*, againft which the beft precautions poffible were

taken

taken in this treaty, which was what made it most acceptable to us.

Yet with all these appearances of mutual benefit, this treaty was no sooner transmitted to the governor of *Barbadoes*, than it produced a misunderstanding. For he, in obedience to his instructions, having caused the substance of it to be proclaimed in *Dominica*, *St. Lucia*, and *St. Vincent*, as members of his government, the *French* took exceptions at that, and questioned our right to any of these islands. They insisted, that they had a claim to *St. Lucia*, and that *Dominica* and *St. Vincent* belonged to the native *Caribbees*, who were under their protection. Upon this a new negotiation arose, conformable to the spirit and letter of the treaty, and in virtue of the king's instructions, the government of *Barbadoes* warmly insisted upon, and exhibited the proofs necessary to establish the rights of the crown of *Great Britain* to all the three islands, as we shall in speaking to those islands shew particularly.

The *French*, in taking upon them to be the protectors of the native *Indians*, adopted the *Spanish* maxim. For though the *Spaniards* had extirpated all the natives, in the great *Antilles* which they possessed, yet upon other nations coming into the *West-Indies*, found it expedient, so stile them their allies, and under that title to assist them, in maintaining their possession in the other isles, to frustrate the endeavours of the *English*, *French*, and *Dutch*, to settle and plant them;

them; and the *French* after they became masters of *Guadaloupe*, and *Martinique*, as they made no scruple of destroying and expelling the inhabitants, so when that was once done, they under colour of a treaty pretended themselves to be under an obligation of defending them in *Dominica* and *St. Vincents*, that they might hinder us from extending our territories, 'till they should grow strong enough to occupy these as they had done the rest.

The negotiation last mentioned, was actually depending, when the revolution happened. But notwithstanding this, the *French*, thinking the opportunity favourable, broke without ceremony the treaty of neutrality, by attacking the *English* quarters in the island of *St. Christopher's*, which, as we have already observed, was insisted upon by King *William* and Queen *Mary*, as the grounds of declaring war against the *French* King in *America*. From this period, down to the treaty of *Aix-la-Chapelle*, both nations have kept up their claims, and by the last mentioned treaty, things were again reduced to their old situation, by a positive declaration that the three islands before-mentioned, should be esteemed neutral; and, considered in that light, not to be settled by either nation. By that treaty likewise, a fourth island was added, to which the *French* had never laid any express or direct claim before, and this was *Tabago*. Such were the regulations this treaty made, and such the state of things, or at least such the state of things ought .

ought to have been, at the opening of the late war. By the *ninth* article of the peace signed at *Paris*, *February* 10, 1763, all the three islands of *Dominica*, *St. Vincents*, and *Tabago*, were yielded in full and perpetual sovereignty to *Great Britain*, the island of *St. Lucia* being ceded by our gracious Sovereign to *France*, in exchange for the island of *Granada*, which by the beforementioned *ninth* Article, together with the *Grenadines* or *Grenadillas*, and all their dependencies, are absolutely and for ever yielded to *Great Britain*. We will therefore, in order to shew what we have obtained in virtue of this peace, first describe the three formerly *neutral*, which are now become *British* islands, and then consider distinctly and at large, the nature and value of the *two Islands*, that were thus exchanged.

DOMINICA lies as it were in the bosom of all the *French* isles, eight leagues north-west from *Martinico*; about the same distance, south-east from *Guadaloupe*; having the three small islands, called *the Saints*, which have been already described, between them; and at the distance of five leagues south-west from *Marigalante*. The island of *Dominica* lies stretched out from south-east to north-west, somewhat resembling in its shape a bent bow, of which, the windward side may be considered as the string. It is a very large fine island, at least twenty-eight *English* miles in length, and full thirteen of our miles in breadth; in circumference, about thirty leagues. It is not broken or intersected by large inlets of
the

the sea, as many others, both of the larger and lesser of our own and the *French West-Indian* islands are, and of course contains the more ground. Some have judged, that it is about twice as big as *Barbadoes*, and the *French* esteem it, to be near half the size of *Martinique*. The air, except in some places that are marshy and over-grown with wood, is generally reputed wholsome, as a proof of which the first *Europeans* who visited it report, that it was at that time very populous, and that the inhabitants were the tallest, best shaped, and at the same time the most robust, active, and warlike of all the *Caribbee Indians*. It may perhaps be thought an additional argument, in support of the salubrity of the air, that *P. Labat* saw Mrs. *Warner* here, who had lived with, and had many children by Sir *Thomas Warner* our first governor in *St. Christophers*, and this so late as in 1700, when she was upwards of one hundred years of age. It is true, he says she was bent double, but at the same time allows her eyes were still very quick, and that she had most of her teeth. There is no doubt, that when this island is cleared, it will like the rest become still more healthy, or at least more agreeable to *European* constitutions.

The face of the country is rough and mountainous, more especially towards the sea side, but within land, there are many rich and fine vallies, and some large and fair plains. The declivities of the hills are commonly gentle, so as to facilitate their cultivation, and the soil almost every

every where a deep black mould, and thence very highly commended for its fertility, by the *Spanish*, *English*, and *French*, who have had occasion and opportunity to examine it; and upon whose concurrent testimonies therefore, we may safely rely. It is excellently well watered, by at least thirty rivers, some, and particularly one of which, is very large and navigable for several miles, the rest very commodious for all the purposes of planting, and abounding with a variety of fine fish. There is a sulphur mountain here, like that in *Martinico*, but not so high, and not far from the sea, rise two hot springs, which upon trial, our countrymen have reported, to be as salutary in their effects as those of *Bath*. In respect to its produce, it abounds with all the kinds of valuable timber, that are to be met with in any of the *West-India* islands, and all of these are excellent in their respective kinds, as the *French* know by experience, and have derived great benefit from them. The fruits likewise, by their confession, are superior to those in *Martinico* and *Guadaloupe*. Hogs both wild and tame are here in great plenty, as well as all sorts of fowls, and for what are called ground provisions, such as bananas, potatoes, manioc, from whence the *Cassada* is made, which is the common bread of the *Indians*, *Negroes*, and even of the *Europeans*, none of the islands produce better, and their pine apples are reputed to be extraordinary large and of the finest flavour. The settlements made by the *French* upon the coast,

coast, were in all respects equal, if not superior in their produce, to those in any of their own islands. The *Spanish* writers, particularly *Oviedo*, say, there are several safe ports and convenient creeks; the *French* for reasons that may be easily guessed, positively assert there are no ports at all. But we know, that at the north-west end of the island, there is a very deep, sandy, spacious bay, well defended by the adjacent mountains from most winds, which, from Prince *Rupert*'s anchoring in it, when in these parts, has received his name, where our armament under Lord *Cathcart*, lay very commodiously, and which was of great service to our squadrons in the course of the late war. Besides, it is out of all dispute, that there is good anchoring ground along all the *Leeward Coast*, and when the island comes to be more thoroughly known, and better examined by our seamen, there is little reason to doubt, that farther conveniences in this respect will be discovered, and if they are capable of it improved.

This island was discovered by Admiral *Columbus*, on *Sunday, November* 3, 1493, and from thence received the name of *Dominica*. But except putting a few hogs upon it, the *Spaniards* did little more than give it a name, and the natural strength of the island with the martial spirit of its inhabitants, rendered it early the principal retreat of the *Caribbees*. In 1596, the Earl of *Cumberland*'s squadron touched here; it was then very well inhabited, and our countrymen
appear

appear to have been kindly received, and courteously entertained by those people. In 1606, the honourable Mr. *George Percy*, brother to the Earl of *Northumberland*, bound with a supply of people to the colony of *Virginia*, came likewise hither. Thus it appears to have been well known to the *English*, long before the *French* had any thing to do in these parts, and therefore we need not wonder that this island as well as many others was inserted in the Earl of *Carlisle*'s patent, or at its being constantly included in every commission granted in succeeding times to the governors of *Barbadoes*. *William*, Lord *Willoughby* of *Parham*, in pursuance of his instructions, sent people to settle there, and appointed a lieutenant governor, and upon some injuries done to the *English* by the natives, he sent an armed force there in 1668, by which they were obliged to submit, and by a solemn instrument surrendered their island to the *English*, and acknowledged themselves subjects to the crown of *Great Britain*; which instrument as appears by the public papers of the island of *Barbadoes*, was delivered to *Edward Littleton*, Esq; then his lordship's secretary. About four year after this (*A. D.* 1672) the *French* first openly disputed our right to this island, under pretence of a peace made by them with the *Indians* in 1640, and as they alledged made at the same time by us. But the council of trade and plantations, by a letter dated *December* the 11th, 1672, acquainted the governor of *Barbadoes*, that never any such treaty existed. Colonel *Thomas Warner*, son to Sir *Thomas Warner*, by the *Indian* woman before-mentioned, continued lieutenant governor there, by commission from the governor of *Barbadoes*, till the time of his death which happened in 1674. In the reign of King *James* II. after the conclusion of the before-mentioned treaty of neutrality with *France*, colonel *Stede* then lieutenant governor of *Barbadoes*, afterwards Sir *Edwin Stede* of *Stede-hill* in the parish of *Harrietsham* in *Kent*, caused that treaty to be proclaimed here, as in an island dependant upon, or rather comprehended within his government; and the following year burned the huts of some *Frenchmen* who had settled on the coast, and seized a ship of the same nation, that was carrying on a trade, and had been cutting wood and taking in water without leave first obtained from the *English*. But King *James* having afterwards signed an act of neutrality, in order to the settling all disputes, by the same ministers who had negotiated the treaty, in consequence thereof sent instructions to that gentleman to transmit the foundations of his Majesty's claim to this and the rest of the islands, inserted in his commission. Accordingly, in obedience to this instruction, after a strict enquiry made, and numerous depositions taken, such a report, bearing date *September* 23, 1688, was actually signed; from which, to use that gentleman's own words, it did fully appear, that the crown of *Britain* had a sole and undoubted right to this, and the rest of of the islands that then were, and constantly had been inserted in his commission. After the treaty of *Ryswic*, we resumed our claim, and attempted to make a settlement. But then, as we are informed by *P. Labat*, the *French* burned our huts, and obliged the people to withdraw. By the treaty of *Aix-la-Chapelle* in 1748, this island was declared neutral; and yet, though the *French* never claimed, or pretended to claim any right to or property in it, when it was reduced by our forces under the command of Lord *Rollo* in 1759, he found almost the whole *Windward Coast* settled by the *French*. But now in virtue of the late treaty, signed at *Paris*, as before has been mentioned, all cavils and disputes are totally and for ever removed, and this island is absolutely ceded and guaranteed to the crown of *Great Britain*; so that our ancient rights are thereby fully and authentically acknowledged, and this isle of *Dominica*, is as much a part of his Majesty's territories, as any other island we possess in the *West-Indies*.

It is evident from the foregoing history, that notwithstanding all the pretences of the *French* to disinterestedness in their opposition to to our claim, as if this proceeded solely from their good faith, in respect to their treaty with the *Indians*, made during our domestic troubles, when the *English* had no support from home; their true and real design, was silently and surreptitiously to occupy this island themselves, as soon as it should be in their power. At the beginning

ginning of this century, as we have seen, the natives were very numerous, and in that state the *French* availed themselves of their alliance, and as we shall see in another place fomented their hatred, and encouraged their expeditions against us, which answered two ends, it rendered it impracticable for our people to form any settlement except by force, and contributed to diminish them as it exposed those *Indians* to our resentment. By the close of the century the *French* writers inform us these poor people were reduced to about two, or at most three thousand souls, and at present there is not a tenth part of that number upon the island. The *French* who from their situation knew much better than we could do, the declining state of the *Caribbee* nation, have been for forty years past, gradually settling along the *Windward Coast*, extending their plantations within land, and, if the the last war had not given us an opportunity to prevent them, would most certainly have executed their project, notwithstanding their alliance with the *Indians*, notwithstanding our claim solemnly acknowledged by those *Indians* with which they were well acquainted, and notwithstanding their several treaties of neutrality. We may therefore, considering things in this light, look upon the acquisition of the island of *Dominico*, as an actual conquest from the *French*, and the state of their plantations, though not very large or considerable, will sufficiently enable us to judge of the value of this country, since they shew us, that sugar, cotton, coffee, cacao, and indeed every thing, that either they or we have been able to raise, in any of the other islands, may be produced in large quantities as well as in the highest degree of perfection here; and, if we consider the size and the situation of this isle, compared either with their possessions or with our own, we may easily estimate the future worth of this country, if properly cultivated by our countrymen abroad, and the interests of those planters vigorously and constantly attended to by government at home.

But it may possibly be surmized, that its situation, as it is before described, is rather a circumstance that may be liable to objection, than any object of commendation, as great danger and difficulty may be from thence apprehended in the settling it. Upon a strict review however, these dangers and difficulties, which some have thought alarming, will not appear to be so very great. In the first place, we have already troops in that part of the world, which upon our evacuating our present conquests, will be sufficient to occupy it. As for the *Indians*, there is no need of removing them, they may for the present, without the least prejudice to our people, have a convenient district of land allotted to them; in which, by prudent management and mild treatment, they may in raising stock and in other things, be made very useful to the new colony, as for a century past they have been to the *French* in *Martinico*, who will feel and regret their loss.

It may be very proper on our firſt eſtabliſhment to allot ſmall plantations, to ſuch ſoldiers, and if they could be found, larger ſhares to ſuch officers, as have families and are inclined to ſettle upon the iſland, and to afford them every kind of encouragement, that may increaſe their number, as thoſe people would be moſt willing, as well as able to defend their property. Numbers of our countrymen ſettled in *St. Euſtatia, St. Croiz,* and at *Cape Iſaquepe,* might be invited to return upon advantageous terms into the territories of their natural Sovereign. A form of government modelled upon thoſe of our other iſlands, guarded againſt the acquiſition, by all-graſping individuals, of large quantities of unſettled and uncultivated land, with thoſe reſtrictions, that take place in *Barbadoes,* for the conſtant maintenance of a numerous and well diſciplined militia, and ſuch other improvements, as thoſe who are the beſt judges of theſe matters may ſuggeſt, could not fail of drawing thither, and that too in a ſhort time, a ſufficient number of inhabitants, and with the help of regular fortifications, and a competent military force ſo long as it ſhould remain neceſſary, with the aſſiſtance of a ſmall naval ſtrength, would in a very ſhort ſpace render the iſland ſecure, and this alone would be ſufficient to render it flouriſhing, which once effected, would attract ſtill greater numbers thither, in hopes of bettering their fortunes. We are the rather induced to hope this, becauſe many inſtances might be given,

given, where with much less encouragement than might be afforded here, and far less security, they have been tempted to seat themselves in other places, and this too under the precarious protection of foreign potentates, and with manifest prejudice to the interests of their mother country, BRITAIN.

If the old possessors of *Dominica*, the *Indians*, barely assisted by the natural strength of the country, while they were at all numerous, were able to preserve their freedom and independency, surrounded as they were with enemies on every side, surely under an attentive and prudent government, advantageous to every settlement, but absolutely necessary in a new colony, the *British* inhabitants settling here, might be very soon put into a condition to protect themselves. Under such a government, the few remaining *Indians*, as has been already suggested, but which can never be too frequently inculcated, would find themselves as much at their ease, and derive more assistance from it, than they ever did from the *French*, and of consequence become more attached to its interest. This possibly, if wisely managed, might induce them to discover that mine, for which the island has been always famous, which the *English* believe from tradition, and report, to be silver; but which the *French* very well know to be gold; and, though very probably it may not be expedient to open it, yet the knowledge of it could not do us any hurt, and the very fame of it, might
invite

invite people, and in time possibly do us good. In case of a war, with the apprehensions of which some people fright themselves, this new acquisition would most certainly be in no danger, for besides the immediate assistance it might receive from *Barbadoes*, while we retain our superiority at sea, a respectable squadron upon the first appearance of a rupture, might be sent to Prince *Rupert*'s bay, with a force sufficient to quiet the fears of the inhabitants. But, if as is much more probable, such an event be at great distance, the island in that time will be fully settled, and from its extent and fortifications out of all jeopardy, from any sudden invasion, and in that state would serve as a place of arms, and the rendezvous of our forces, from all parts of the *West-Indies*, when from the nature of its situation the whole of the *French* commerce must instantly become precarious, and all their settlements in a very short space, be entirely at our mercy. A circumstance, which as we shall hereafter have occasion to remark, the *French* in the *West-Indies*, who in this respect are the best judges, have always foreseen; and therefore very justly dreaded.

We come now to the island of *St. Vincent*, which lies between five and six leagues south-west from *St. Lucia*; twenty-three south-west from *Martinico*; thirty-six south from *Dominica*; thirty west by south from *Barbadoes*; and seventeen north-east from *Granada*. Being thus situated, directly to the leeward of *Barbadoes*, it it may in a few hours be reached from thence, and is at the same time so seated, as to cover and connect the small islands that lie between it and *Granada*. It is said by *de Laet*, to have a great resemblance to the island of *Ferro*, which is one of the *Canaries*; but this is to be understood of the aspect of the country, rather than of its shape. It is from south to north, about twenty-four of our miles in length, and about half as many in breadth, sixty, or it may be something more in circumference. In point of size, it is rather bigger than *Antigua*, if not larger, at least as large as *Barbadoes*, somewhat smaller than *St. Lucia*, and much about two thirds of the bigness of *Dominica*. It is necessary to state its situation and extent circumstantially, not only to shew its importance more certainly, as well as more clearly, but also as we may have occasion to have recourse to this account, when we come to speak of that neutral isle that we have ceded. The warmth of the climate, is so tempered by the sea breezes, that it is looked upon as very healthy and agreeable, and on the eminencies which are numerous the air is rather cool.

The soil is wonderfully fertile, tho' the country is hilly, and in some places mountainous. But amongst the former, there are very pleasant vallies, and at the bottom of the latter, some spacious and luxuriant plains. No island of the same extent is better watered, for from the mountains there descend rivers, and lesser streams

run

run on both sides from almost every hill. There are several fine springs at a small distance from the sea, and the slopes are so easy and regular, that there are hardly any marshes, and no standing waters in the isle. There are here great quantites of fine timber, and excellent fruit-trees, some peculiar to this island. It abounds with wild sugar-canes, from which the natives make a very pleasant liqour; corn, rice, and all sorts of ground provision, are raised in plenty, and with little trouble. In the south part of the island, where the *French* have raised some spacious and flourishing settlements; they have coffee, indigo, cacao, anotta, and very fine tobacco. They likewise raise abundance of cattle and poultry, and send from thence *lignum vitæ*, and other kinds of timber to *Martinico*, where they are employed in building houses, and in their fortifications. The rivers are stored with various kinds of fresh fish, and the sea near its coasts abounds with those proper to that element. Here are also both land and water fowl in plenty. We may therefore from these specimens collect, that if this country were thoroughly and regularly cultivated, it would in respect to its produce, be very little if at all inferior, to any of the islands that we already possess; more especially, if we consider that it has many commodious bays, on the north-west and south-west sides, with abundance of convenient creeks, and good anchoring ground on every side. At the southern extremity there is a deep, spacious, sandy

sandy bay, called in the old charts the bay of *St. Antonio*, where ships of large size may lie very safely and commodiously, and when it is better and more thoroughly known, other advantages may probably be discovered, for hitherto we have no good description of it by any *English* writer, and the *French* take care to represent it, as an insignificant disagreeable desart.

The *Spaniards* bestowed the name it has ever born upon this island, because they discovered it upon the twenty-second of *January*, which is *St. Vincents*'s day in their Calendar, but it does not appear they were ever properly speaking in possession of it, the *Indians* being very numerous here, on account of its being the rendezvous of their expeditions to the continent. It was frequently visited by the *English* in the beginning of the last century, when they had their northern and *Guiana* settlements in view, which was the reason of its being inserted in the Earl of *Carlisle*'s patent, who certainly intended settling all the islands therein mentioned, and might possibly have effected it, if our civil wars had not interfered. In a little time after the restoration, when that Earl's patent was surrendered, King *Charles* II. granted to *Francis*, Lord *Willoughby* of *Parham*, a commission to be Governor and Captain General of *Barbadoes* and all the *Leeward Islands*, which he held to his death, and being lost in a storm going on an expedition against the *Dutch*, towards the latter end of the month of *July* 1666, the King was pleased to grant

grant the like commission, to his brother *William,* Lord *Willoughby,* who was very careful in maintaining the rights of his government, which induced him in 1668 to send a force thither; when as *P. du Tetre* very frankly owns, he re-established the *English* government, which the *Indians* had rejected, and obliged those of *St. Vincents* as well as of *Dominica,* to acknowledge themselves subjects to the crown of *Great Britain.*

In 1672, King *Charles* thought fit to divide these governments, and by a new commission appointed Lord *Willoughby* Governor of *Barbadoes, St. Lucia, St. Vincent,* and *Dominica*; Sir *William Stapleton* being appointed Governor of the other *Leeward Isles,* and this separation has subsisted ever since, the same islands being constantly inserted, in every new governor's patent. On the demise of Lord *Willoughby,* Sir *Jonathan Atkins,* was appointed Governors of *Barbadoes* and the rest of these islands, and so continued till 1680, when he was succeeded by Sir *Richard Dutton,* who being sent for into *England* in 1685, appointed Colonel *Edwin Stede* Lieutenant Governor, who vigorously asserted our rights by appointing Deputy Governors for the other islands; and particularly sent Captain *Temple* hither, to prevent the *French* from wooding and watering, without our permission, to which they had been encouraged, by the inattention of the former governors, persisting steadily in this conduct, till it was signified to him, as we have had occasion

casion to remark before, that the King had signed an act of neutrality, and that commissioners were appointed, by the two courts, to settle all differences relative to these islands.

Some years after, a ship from *Guinea*, with a large cargo of slaves, was either wrecked or run on shore upon the island of *St. Vincent*, into the woods and mountains of which, great numbers of the *Negroes* escaped. Here whether willingly or unwillingly is a little incertain, the *Indians* suffered them to remain, and partly by the accession of run away slaves from *Barbadoes*, partly by the children they had by the *Indian* women, they became very numerous; so that about the beginning of the current century, they constrained the *Indians* to retire into the north-west part of the island. These people as may be reasonably supposed, were much dissatisfied with this treatment, and complained of it occasionally, both to the *English* and to the *French*, that came to wood and water amongst them. The latter, at length suffered themselves to be prevailed upon, to attack these invaders, in the cause of their old allies; and from a persuasion that they should find more difficulty in dealing with these *Negroes*, in case they were suffered to strengthen themselves, than with the *Indians*. After much deliberation, in the year 1719, they came with a considerable force from *Martinico*, and landing without much opposition, began to burn the *Negroes* huts, and destroy their plantations, supposing that the *Indians*

*dians* would have attacked them in the mountains, which if they had done, the *Blacks* had probably been extirpated, or forced to submit and become slaves. But either from fear or policy, the *Indians* did nothing, and the *Negroes* sallying in the night, and retreating to inaccessible places in the day, destroyed so many of the *French* (amongst whom was Mr. *Paulian*, Major of *Martinique*, who commanded them) that they were forced to retire. When by this experiment, they were convinced that force would not do, they had recourse to fair means, and by dint of persuasions and presents, patched up a peace with the *Negroes* as well as the *Indians*, from which they received great advantage.

Things were in this situation, when Captain *Uring*, came with a considerable armament, to take possession of *St. Lucia* and this island, in virtue of a grant from our late Sovereign King *George* I. to the late Duke of *Montague*, of which we shall have occasion to speak again hereafter. When the *French* had dislodged this gentleman, by a superior force, from *St. Lucia* he sent Captain *Braithwaite*, to try what could be done, at the island of *St. Vincent*, in which he was not at all more successful, as will best appear from that gentleman's report to Mr. *Uring*, which as it contains several curious circumstances, relative to the country and to the two independant nations who then inhabited it, belongs properly to this subject, and cannot but prove entertaining to the reader. The paper

is

[ 97 ]

is without date, but it appears from Mr. *Uring*'s memoirs, that this transaction happened in the spring of the year 1723.

## THE REPORT.

"In pusuance of a resolution in council and your order for so doing, the day you sailed with his Grace's colony for *Antego*, I sailed with the *Griffin* sloop, in company with his Majesty's ship the *Winchelsea* to *St. Vincent*. We made the island that night, and next morning run along shore, and saw several *Indian* huts, but as yet no *Indians* came off to us, nor could we get ashore to them, by reason there was no ground to anchor in. Towards the evening, two *Indians* came on board and told us, we might anchor in a bay to leeward, and when we were at anchor, they would bring their general on board. Here we came to an anchor in deep water, and very dangerous for the sloop. One whom they called *General* came on board, with several others, to the number of twenty two. I entertained them very handsomely, and made the chief some trifling presents, but found he was a person of no consequence, and that they called him *Chief*, to get some present from me. Here two of the *Indians* were so drunk they would not go ashore, but stay'd on board some days, and were well entertained. After this, little winds and great

"curents

"curents drove us off for several days; but
"at last we came to an anchor in a spacious
"bay, to leeward of all the island, the draught
"of which I ordered to be taken by our sur-
"veyor, for your better understanding the
"place, being the only one, where a settle-
"ment could be made. The ship and sloop
"were scarce come to an anchor, before the
"strand of the shore was covered with *Indians*,
"and amongst them we could discover a white,
"who proved to be a *Frenchman*. I took
"Captain *Watson* in the boat with me, with a
"*Frenchman*, and immediately went ashore.
"As soon as I came amongst them, I asked
"why they appeared all armed? For every
"man had cutlasses, some had musquets, pis-
"tols, bows, and arrows, &c. They with
"very little ceremony inclosed me, and carried
"me up the country, about a mile, over a
"little rivulet, where I was told I was to see
"their general. I found him, sitting amidst a
"guard of about a hundred *Indians*, those
"nearest his person had all musquets, the rest
"bows and arrows, and great silence. He or-
"dered me a seat, and a *Frenchman* stood at
"his right-hand, for an interpreter: he de-
"manded of me, what brought me into his
"country, and of what nation? I told him
"*English*, and I was put in to wood and water,
"as not caring to say any thing else before the
"*Frenchman*; but told him if he would be
"pleased to come on board our ships, I would
"leave

"leave *Englishmen* in hostage for him, and those
"he should be pleased to bring with him; but
"I could not prevail with him, either to come
"on board or suffer me to have wood and
"water. He said, he was informed we were
"come to force a settlement, and we had no
"other way to remove that jealousy, but to
"get under sail. As soon as I found what in-
"fluence the *Frenchman*'s company had upon
"them, I took my leave after making such
"replies, as I thought proper, and returned
"to my boat, under a guard. When I came to
"the shore, I found the guard there were in-
"creased by a number of *Negroes*, all armed
"with fuzees. I got in my boat, without any
"any injury, and went on board to Captain
"*Orme* and told him my ill success."

"Immediately after I sent on shore, the
"sloop's boat with a mate, with rum, beef,
"and bread, &c. with some cutlasses, and or-
"dered a *Frenchman* who went with the mate,
"to desire the guard to conduct them to their
"general, and to tell him that tho' he denied
"me the common good of water and a little
"useless wood; nevertheless I had sent him
"such refreshments, as our ships afforded.
"Our people found the *Frenchman* gone, and
"that then the *Indian* general seemed pleased,
"and received what was sent him, and in re-
"turn sent me bows and arrows."

"Our people had not been long returned,
"but their general sent a canoe with two chief
"*Indians,*

" *Indians*, who spoke very good *French*, to
" thank me for my presents, and to ask par-
" don for his refusing me wood and water, and
" assured me I might have what I pleased, and
" they had orders to tell me, if I pleased to
" go ashore again, they were to remain hostages
" for my civil treatment. I sent them on board
" the man of war, and with Captain *Watson*
" went on shore. I was well received, and con-
" ducted as before. But now I found the bro-
" ther of the chief of the *Negroes*, was arrived
" with five hundred *Negroes*, most armed with
" fuzees. They told my interpreter, they were
" assured we were come to force a settlement,
" or else they would not have denied me what
" they never before denied any *English*, viz.
" wood and water. But, if I pleased, I might
" take in what I wanted under a guard. Find-
" ing them in so good a humour, I once more
" introduced the desire I had to entertain them
" on board our ships, and with some difficulty,
" prevailed with them, by leaving Capt. *Watson*
" on shore under their guard, as a hostage. I
" carried them on board the King's ship, where
" they were well entertained by Captain *Orme*,
" who gave the *Indian* general a fine fuzee
" of his own, and to the chief of the *Ne-*
" *groes* something that pleased him. Captain
" *Orme* assured him of the friendship of the
" King of *England*, &c. The *Negroe* chief
" spoke excellent *French*, and gave answers with
" the *French* complements. Afterwards I car-
" ried

"ried them on board the Duke's sloop, and
" after opening their hearts with wine, for they
" scorned to drink rum, I thought it a good
" time to tell them my commission, and what
" brought me upon their coast. They told me
" it was well I had not mentioned it ashore,
" for their power could not have protected me;
" that it was impossible; the *Dutch* had before
" attempted it, but were glad to retire. They
" likewise told me two *French* sloops had the
" day before we came, been amongst them,
" gave them arms and ammunition, and assur-
" ed them of the whole force of *Martinico* for
" their protection against us. They told them
" also that they had drove us from *St. Lucia*,
" and that now we were come to endeavour to
" force a settlement there, and notwithstanding
" all our specious pretences, when we had
" power, we should enslave them, but declared
" they would trust no *Europeans*, that they
" owned themselves under the protection of the
" *French*, but would as soon oppose their set-
" tling amongst them, or any act of force from
" them, as us, as they had lately given an ex-
" ample, by killing several; and they further
" told me, it was by very large presents, the
" *French* ever got in their favour again, but
" they resolved never to put it in their power,
" or any *European* to hurt them. They ad-
" vised me, to think what they said was an
" act of friendship. This being all I could get
" from them, I dismissed them, with such pre-

" sents as his grace ordered for that service;
" with a discharge of cannon, and received in
" return, as regular vollies of small shot, as I
" ever heard. In the night, the *Winchelsea*
" drove from her anchors, which as soon as I
" perceived, and had received Captain *Watson*
" from the shore, I got under sail and stood
" to the man of war."

There is nothing said in this paper, that can lead us in any tolerable degree, to compute the numbers either of the *Negroes* or the *Indians*, but Captain *Uring* in his map of the *West-Indies*, probably from the best accounts he could collect, says that together they made about twelve hundred. In spite of the assurances they gave him, and notwithstanding the attempts which the *French* had made to destroy them, it was not long before they suffered some of that nation to settle about the great bay, in the south part of the island, from whence in the space of about sixteen years, they gradually spread along the coast, till at length they fixed themselves in every bay, and at the mouth of every river, almost throughout the island. In the year 1735, it appeared by an authentic report, that was then made to the government of *Barbadoes*, that according to the best information, which could be at that juncture obtained, there were about six hundred *French*, four thousand *Indians*, and six thousand *Negroes* in *St. Vincents*. But if any credit be due to the reports, that have been since recieved from masters of ships who have frequented

frequented the *West-Indies*, hostilities having some time after broke out between the *Indians* and the *Negroes*, they have carried on for several years a most cruel and continual war against each other; in which so many have been slain, that it is thought both nations are at this time very much decreased in their numbers. This dissention between them, must have been very advantageous of course to the *French*, who have gone on settling, planting, cutting timber, and raising every kind of *West-India* commodity, except sugar, and carrying on a very lucrative trade to their other islands, in which a number of sloops have been employed, while under colour of protecting their allies, the inhabitants of our colonies have been excluded from all the benefits they formerly received from this island, at least in a great measure, for it must be neverthelefs acknowledged whenever either the *Indians* or the *Negroes* have had it in their power, they have traded as readily, and afforded their assistance as willingly to the subjects of *Great Britain* as to the *French*. Thus the reader has seen the history of *St. Vincent* and its inhabitants, both *Indians* and *Negroes*, as truly and as succinctly set down, as it could be obtained, and upon this it may not be amiss to make a few general remarks.

The *Caribbee Indians*, and the independent *Negroes*, ought from principles of policy as well as justice to lose nothing by their change of protectors. The *British* government will certainly preserve to them all that they have hitherto enjoyed,

joyed, restore peace between them, and by giving them security in the possession of their little dwellings, acquire a number of new and useful subjects, which in all countries, and in these especially, are of more consequence than extent of territory. It is well-known, that the *Indians* are very adroit in raising poultry, as well as in many other respects, when treated with lenity and indulgence; as the *Negroes* are in cultivating all kinds of ground provisions, as well as in fowling, hunting, and fishing. By these employments to which they are naturally addicted, as well as by many others, they have been for a long series of years, as the inhabitants of our plantations well know, very serviceable to the *French*, who took care to reward their services with such things as were most agreeable to them; and which, no doubt, will be as well received from us. Their assistance in these respects as it may facilitate the speedy establishment of a compact and respectable body of *British* settlers, by diminishing their otherwise necessary attention to these and such like smaller concerns, would be exceedingly beneficial to a new colony, and when they shall have experienced the justice, moderation, and equity of a *British* government, they will not only be reconciled to, but become sensible also of their being gainers by the alteration, and from thence become thoroughly attached to our interests, as finding them inseparably and perpetually blended with their own.

If it should be objected, that their former conduct seems however to shew the contrary; the answer is equally easy and decisive. The circumstances of things by which that was occasioned, are now entirely changed, and as it is an invariable maxim with the *Indians*, to adhere to the strongest, they will certainly quit the *French*, when they see they have made no scruple of quitting them. On the other hand, the *Negroes* are ever true to their own interests, without being at all slow in apprehending them, and if they receive the like or greater encouragements from *British* subjects, for their voluntary assistance in bringing provisions, felling timber, &c. than they did from the *French*, they will most certainly prefer freedom with these advantages, to what must otherwise certainly prove their last resource, leaving the island retiring to and remaining amongst the *French*, and submitting to them, and so gradually becoming slaves. If these reasons are not sufficient to convince, let us have recourse to facts. Our countrymen in *Jamacia*, have felt no inconveniences, but quite the contrary (since those people are now regarded as making a part of the strength of that island) from the peace they made with their free *Negroes*. Besides, we see that notwithstanding the professions both of the *Indians* and the *Negroes* in this very island, they have actually allowed the *French* to settle amongst them, and to raise very fine plantations; and, if the *French* lived in peace and with security amongst them, without any regular establishment, or force to protect them, why with the assistance of both, may not we? There is no doubt, that a competent military force must be sent to protect our first establishments, and as assistance may be derived from *Barbadoes* at any time in the space of a few hours, these people can never be formidable to a *British* colony, though by a wise and prudent administration, they may be made very subservient and useful to it, more especially, when our taking possession of this country is so clear and incontestable a proof of our superiority, an argument of all others the most conclusive to these people, and by the opinion of which alone, they were for half a century past attached to the *French*, and not from any prediliction in favour of that nation.

But even supposing, which however it is unjust to suppose, there were still any weight in this objection. The evil is not without the reach of remedy; for the *Indians* may be removed to one end of the island, and the *Negroes* left at the other. If even this should not be judged sufficient, the *Indians* may be transported to their countrymen in *Dominica*, which country being so much larger, and having but very few *Indians* in it, they could not then be very dangerous; or if this expedient should not be relished, the *Indians* in this island and in *Dominica*, may be sent into some of the islands in the *Granadillas*, which they now frequently visit, and where they might live in their own way, under our protection, and at such a distance from the *French*, as to remove all kinds of jealousy of

their

their being excited by them to give us any kind of difturbance. The *Negroes* by this diminution of ftrength, would be lefs able and perhaps lefs inclined, to rifk the advantages they might derive from our protection, for the miferies of flavery, or the chance of being fold to the *Spaniards*, to work in their mines, the evil in the world, of which (and with great juftice) they are moft apprehenfive.

This in itfelf, from the foregoing defcription, appears unqueftionably to be a very fine and fertile ifland. All the ancient and of courfe unbiaffed relations we have of it by authors of every nation, *Spanifh*, *French*, and *Dutch*, as well as our own, concur in this affertion. The number of inhabitants who lived folely upon its produce, and yet were fo far from being ftraitned for any of the neceffaries of life, that they were always in a condition to fupply ftrangers with whatever they wanted, is a concurrent proof of this, fo that confidered fimply in this point of view, our eftablifhing our ancient rights to *St. Vincent* by the late peace, ought to be confidered as a very valuable acquifition. Nor is this at all diminifhed by its having inhabitants upon it, but quite the contrary, fince they may have fpace enough to purfue their former manner of living, without any prejudice to our fettlements, for the reafons that have been already given; and, therefore, if this can be brought about, it will be a great additional advantage, as it may poffibly afford us the means of difcovering, how blacks may be rendred active and
induftrious

industrious who are not slaves. In the mean time it is, as we have already observed, a very convincing proof of its being both a wholesome and a fruitful country, for otherwise the *Indians* might easily have quitted it, to retire to their countrymen in *Dominica*; or the *Negroes*, if they had thought they could have exchanged it for the better, might without any great difficulty have possessed themselves at least in part of *St. Lucia*; and that neither of these nations were inclined to the taking such a step, seems to be a conclusive argument, that they preferred this to any other island, and whatever their motives for that might be, those motives are certainly favourable with respect to the idea we ought to form of this country, and so far ought to weigh with us, not to think lightly of it, or in any degree to induce a persuasion that the *French*, from their knowledge of both islands, chose to leave us the worst.

We may be the more clearly convinced of the reality of this observation, by adverting to the certain, indeed to the avowed design of the *French*, which was gradually to seize and occupy all these islands, not only with a view to benefit themselves, but also at the same time to straiten and distress us. We may therefore regard the recovering our right to and possession of *St. Vincent* as well as we before remarked in respect to *Dominica*, in the light of an actual conquest from the *French*, as much as if we had retained any other of their islands. For

by

by our poffeffing *St. Vincent*, we plainly deprive them of all the fettlements they had made there, of the produce of thofe fettlements, and of the advantages arifing from the trade, which was already fettled between this and their other iflands, which was continually increafing, and confequently adding to their wealth and ftrength. We have alfo deprived them of their *Indian* and *Negroe* allies, who by this ceffion become inconteftibly our fubjects, which is not only a lofs to them, but a benefit to us. Add to all this, that we deprive them of the power, which in confequence of their plantations upon the ifland, and the protection they gave to the *Indians* and *Negroes* therein, they had acquired of difturbing our colonies, and diftreffing our navigation, which they never failed to do to the greateft degree poffible. This is of fo much the greater confequence, as though thefe hardfhips in time of peace, in direct violation of treaties, and more efpecially of the laft treaty of *Aix-la-Chapelle*, were fufficiently known and felt, and became thereby the foundation of repeated complaints; yet for the fake of maintaining peace, and the apprehenfions of entering into an expenfive war, on difputes that were thought in comparifon with that expence of little confequence, our fubjects entertained fmall hopes of redrefs. The cafe is now quite altered; this ifland is become perpetually and inconteftibly ours, and the *French* have no colour or pretence,

tence for reviving, or will be ever suffered to revive any such practices again.

But even this, though a great deal, is not all that may be said, and said with truth, upon this subject. By the acquisition of *St. Vincent*, we have likewise gained a perpetual check upon the *French* islands, and particularly on that of *St. Lucia* which is ceded to them. There can be no measures taken there, of which we may not have immediate notice, and if we consider the situation of this island in respect to that, and the rest of the *French* islands, now that *Granada* and all its dependencies are become ours, it is also apparent we may from thence establish a cruize, by which they will be effectually blocked up, or at least deprived of all commerce, in case of a future war. Nor is it much to the purpose to object, that possibly the bays in this island may not be convenient for a large squadron, since in reality, our squadrons avoid as much as possible coming into or continuing long in bays however commodious, for many and those also very just reasons; nor does experience evince, that our naval armaments have hitherto suffered much from the want of such conveniencies, to which when wanted most, that is in the *Hurricane* months, they would hardly trust, and from which dangerous storms they will, for the future, have a constant and safe retreat, in the ports of *Granada*. It may also serve us for a place of arms, to which forces may be transported

ported from the other islands, and embarked very conveniently for any future expedition. It likewise contributes to cover and connect all our other possessions, that together with it have been acquired by the peace; and from thence reinforcements and supplies may be sent with equal ease and expedition to *Dominica*; so that all circumstances considered, we must be great and perpetual gainers by our having obtained this island, without, as shall be hereafter shewn, feeling any material inconveniences from the cession of *St. Lucia*.

TABAGO, the most remote of our islands, lies near forty leagues south by west from *Barbadoes*, about thirty-five leagues south-east from *St. Vincent*, forty leagues east from *Granada*, twelve leagues north-east from *Trinidada*, and between thirty and forty leagues north-east from the *Spanish* main. According to the latest and most certain accounts of this island, it is thirty-two of our miles from south-east to north-west, which is its greatest length; and where broadest may be about nine miles, from east to west, somewhat more than seventy miles in circumference. It differs not much in bigness from the island of *St. Vincent*, is rather larger than *Barbadoes*, and of consequence than any of our *Leeward Islands*. Near the north-east extremity, there lies a small island called *Little Tabago*, which is near two miles in length, and full half a mile broad. The rocks of *St. Giles* lie to the north, and there are many small rocky islets on the west side of it, which tho' useless are not however at all dangerous.

The

The climate, though it lies only eleven degrees and ten minutes north from the equator, is not near so hot as might be expected, the force of the sun's rays being tempered by the coolness of the sea breeze. When it was first inhabited, it was thought unhealthy, but as soon as it was a little cleared and cultivated, it was found to be equally pleasant and wholesome, which the *Dutch* ascribed in a great measure, to the odoriferous smell exhaled from the spice and rich gum trees, a notion borrowed from their countrymen in the *East-Indies*, who are persuaded that cutting down the clove trees in the *Moluccas* has rendered those islands very unhealthy. There is likewise another circumstance, which may serve to recommend this climate, and that is the island's lying out of the track of the *Hurricanes*, to which our own islands and those of the *French* are exposed, and from which their plantations and shipping suffer frequently very severely.

There are many rising grounds over all the island, but it cannot be properly stiled mountainous, except perhaps in the north-west extremity; and even there, they are far from being rugged or impassable. The soil is very finely diversified, being in some places light and sandy, in others mixed with gravel and small flints, but in general it is a deep, rich, black mold. It is from the extraordinary size of the same sort of trees that grow in the other islands, as well as from the trials made by the *Courlanders* and
the

the *Dutch* esteemed to be luxuriantly fertile, well suited to the different productions that are raised in the *West-Indies*, and from the concurrence of various favourable circumstances, which will be hereafter mentioned, may be wrought with ease, and is not liable to the blast and other accidents, which are so fatal to the most promising crops in some of our *Leeward Islands*.

We find it generally agreed, that hardly any country can be better watered than this is. For besides springs that are found in plenty all over the island, there are not fewer than eighteen rivulets, that run from the hills into the sea, some on the east and some on the west side. Of these, there are some, that take a serpentine course through the meadows; and others that being pent up by rocky channels, roll with such rapidity, as renders them very fit for driving mills, but there are very few or no morasses or marshes, or any lakes, pools, or collections of standing waters, which of course must render it more healthy, and all parts of it alike habitable, and from the happy disposition of the running streams and numerous springs, almost every where habitable, with the like convenience.

Yet this distribution of fresh water, is not at all more commodious, than the disposition of the bays and creeks of the sea upon its coasts. At the south end of the island lies the bay of *La Güira*, and at a small distance from thence the lesser and the greater *Rockley* bays. The latter of these, may with propriety be stiled a harbour,

bour, for it is land-locked on every side, and very secure. It was in this bay the *Dutch* and *French* fleets engaged in 1677, and in which the Count *d'Estrees*'s ship, called the *Glorieux* of seventy guns, was blown up, which shews that it is capable of receiving as considerable squadrons, and those too of as large ships, as are usually sent into these seas. To the northward of these lies *Cochon Gras* or *Fat Hog* bay, and beyond those *Grand Rivier* bay, *Great Hog* bay, *Little Hog* bay, *L'Ance Batteau*, covered by the island of *Little Tabago*; and therefore in the *Dutch* maps called *Little Tabago* bay. Opposite to this, on the other side of the island, is what the *Dutch* called *John Moore*'s bay, now *Man of War* bay, very deep and spacious, with ten fathom water close to the shore, with two fine rivulets running into the bay, where our ships may therefore careen, with the utmost conveniency, as well as with the greatest safety, as it is surrounded by high hills, that come down close to the shore, by which the vessels lying there, will be most effectually sheltered from both wind and weather. There are also several little commodious bays, between this and *Great Courland* bay, which is very spacious, capable of containing a large squadron, with a beautiful level country adjoining to it on the coast, which when cleared may render it a commodious and pleasant habitation. Beyond this, lies *Little Courland* bay, and *Sandy Point* bay, which brings us again to the southern extremity of the island.

island. Hence it appears, that it is in all respects most convenient for commerce, and tho' it be true, that having so many places that admit of easy landing, and lying in the neighbourhood of warlike *Indian* nations, it must of necessity require proper fortifications, the many obvious and extraordinary advantages thereby afforded to trade, when the island shall be once settled, will amply compensate the expence, that may be found necessary to provide for, and to preserve its security.

This island is covered with all that vast variety of valuable timber, that is to be found in most countries in the *West-Indies*, and many of these as extraordinary in their size, as excellent in their nature. The same may be said, with respect to fruit-trees, and amongst these, there are some that are peculiar to *Tabago*. Such for instance as the true *nutmeg-tree*, which the *Dutch*, who of all nations could not in that respect be deceived, affirm to have found here. It is true, they say it is a wild nutmeg, that the *mace* is less florid, and the taste of the nut itself more pungent, though larger and fairer to the eye, than the spice of the same kind brought by them, from the *East-Indies*. The *cinnamon-tree* grows likewise in this island, though the bark is said to have a taste of *cloves* as well as *cinnamon*. Here likewise grows that tree which produces the true *gum copal*, resembling that brought from the continent of *America*, and very different from what goes by the same name in the rest of the *West-India* islands.

All ground provisions are produced here in the utmost abundance, as well as in the highest perfection. Here likewise is plenty of wild hogs and other animals, together with great quantities of fowl, and an amazing variety both of sea and river fish. In the time the *Dutch* were in possession of this island, which was not many years, they exported large quantities of tobacco, sugar, cassia, ginger, cinnamon, sassafras, gum *copal*, cacao, rocou, indigo, and cotton; besides rich woods, materials for dying, drugs of different kinds, and several sorts of delicious sweetmeats. Thus, we have not only the probability, arising from the climate, soil, and situation, but likewise the certainty, that all the valuable commodities which the *West-India* islands produce, have been actually and may consequently be again unquestionably raised in *Tabago*. We may add to this, that though the *Dutch* boasted much of the worth of their settlements in, and the valuable cargoes they annually brought from thence, yet Sir *Josiah Child*, within that very period, mentions the defect in their improvement of *Tabago*, in support of his doctrine, that the *Dutch*, as a nation, were less successful in *planting* than *commerce*; which is enough to convince us, that in his time, this was considered as an island capable of being made at least as valuable, as any of its size in the possession of *Europeans*.

TABAGO

TABAGO was discovered by Admiral *Christopher Columbus* in the year 1498, but it does not appear, that the *Spaniards* ever made any establishment thereon. It was near a century after this, before it became known to us, and this in consequence of the expeditions made in the reign of Queen *Elizabeth* into these parts, against the *Spaniards*, and particularly by that able seaman Sir *Robert Dudley*, who in 1595, took notice of it, as well as of other islands in his expedition to *Trinidada*. It was from this time, that those adventurous *Englishmen*, who meditating the extension of our naval power in the most distant parts of the world, began to entertain thoughts of planting some of the small islands neglected by the *Spaniards*, and *Tabago* amongst the rest. It was with this view, that *William* Earl of *Pembroke*, a nobleman of great merit, who had distinguished himself in contributing to other enterprizes of the like kind, sollicited and obtained in the reign of King *Charles* I. *Anno Domini* 1628, a grant of the islands of *Tabago*, *Barbuda*, and *St. Bernard*. It is incertain whether he ever actually attempted to carry his design into execution, and very possibly the setling them might be hindered by that nobleman's death, which happened in less than two years after. It is not at all however improbable, that he was led to the knowledge of these islands, by the master of some ship of his own, or by the captains of vessels fitted out for other discoveries, in which he had an interest,

tereſt, becauſe as we have already ſhewn, in ſpeaking of the iſland of *St. Chriſtophers*, this was in thoſe days a thing not very extraordinary.

It was not long after this, that ſome ſhips belonging to a company of merchants ſettled in *Zealand*, coming into theſe ſeas, took notice of this iſland, and made ſo full and favourable a report of it, at their return, as induced that company to think of planting it. They ſent accordingly ſome people thither, about 1632, and by that means acquired ſuch lights, as enabled *John de Laet* to give a more copious and much better deſcription of it, than of any of the *Caribbee* iſlands. Theſe *Dutchmen* beſtowed on this their favourite acquiſition, the appellation of *New Walcheren* in honour of the iſland of the ſame name, which was and is one of the moſt conſiderable in the province of *Zealand*. When their ſmall colony was increaſed by repeated ſupplies to the number of about two hundred ſouls, they began to think of erecting a fort for their ſecurity. This was ſo much the more neceſſary, becauſe the country being very eaſy of acceſs, the warlike *Indians* from the continent, frequently paſſed over thither, and the *Caribbee Indians* on the other hand, conſidered it as a convenient place of arms, for aſſembling their forces, when they went to make deſcents upon their enemies territories on the continent. The *Dutch* having made a good progreſs in their fort, held theſe people in great contempt, who thereupon applied themſelves to the *Spaniard:*

*niards* in the ifland of *Trinidada*, who very readily liftened to their follicitations, and fending a competent force to affift thefe *Indians*, the *Dutch* fort not quite finifhed was eafily taken, and the whole of the little colony, according to the barbarous cuftom of thofe people, was utterly deftroyed. This as we have before obferved was very confiftent with the *Spanish* policy, which always leads them to affift the *Indians*, when by fuch a ftep, they can defeat the purpofes of other *European* nations. And thus ended the firft attempt to fettle this ifland.

It was about ten years after this, when this ifle was totally deftitute of inhabitants, that *James* Duke of *Courland* or rather *Curland* who had our King *James* I. for his god-father, and who was a Prince of great enterprize, as well as pregnant abilities, entertained a notion of augmenting the wealth of his fubjects and increafing his own revenue, by making a fettlement in fome of the uninhabited iflands in *America*, and it fo fell out, that the lights he received upon communicating this project, directed his views hither. He fent accordingly a competent number of men well fupplied with every thing for their accommodation, and directed them to begin with providing for their own fecurity. They accordingly fixed themfelves upon that, which has been ever fince called *Great Courland* bay, where with great expedition, they erected a fmall regular fortification; to which in honour of their Sovereign, they gave the name of *James* fort.

fort. When they had done this, they built a little town near it, and keeping up a constant corespendence, and receiving continual supplies from their own country, they in the space of a very few years, cultivated a considerable space round them, and thereby raised a very compact and flourishing colony, living upon so good terms with all their neighbours, and discovering so little inclination to hurt or disturb others, that it does not appear, that either the *Indians* or the *Spaniards* made any attempt to disturb them. Such was the good fortune, arising from the good conduct of this second colony.

Two opulent magistrates of the town of *Flushing*, Messrs. *Adrian* and *Cornelius Lampsins*, being desirous of supporting the honour which their island had acquired, by bestowing its name upon another in the *West-Indies*, fitted out some ships at their expence, which arrived at *Tabago* in 1654, and debarked a considerable number of people. But finding the *Courlanders* in possession, with a good fort and a respectable strength, they judged it better to compromise matters for the present, and to seat themselves on the other side of the island, acknowledging themselves to derive that settlement from, and to hold it under the protection of *James* Duke of *Courland*. The place where they fixed their residence was upon *Rood Klyps*, that is *Redcliff*, now *Rockley* bay, and there by a continual accession of recruits, from their own county, they became very numerous. In the mean time a great misfortune

misfortune happened to the Duke of *Courland*, who notwithstanding the neutrality which had been granted him, during the war between *Sweden* and *Poland*, was by the superior power of *Charles Gustavus* King of *Sweden* dispossessed of his dominions, and himself carried prisoner first to *Riga* and next to *Ivanogorod* in 1658, from a mere motive of policy, or it may be of jealousy, as he had exceedingly improved his country, and raised a respectable marine, his *Swedish* Majesty declaring, that though his cousin of *Courland* was too little to be a King, he was too great to be a Duke. The *Dutch* in *Tabago*, receiving the first news of this unfortunate revolution, immediately took up arms, invested *Fort James*, declared to the *Courlanders* the situation of their Prince, and demanded possession of their fortress and town, promising to restore both, whenever the Duke recovered his liberty. The governor of *Fort James* would have defended it, but his garrison mutinied and forced him to deliver it up; by which the *Dutch* became possessors of the whole island. This revolution happened in 1659 or 1660.

In order to maintain this possession, and at the same time to acquire some colour of title, Mr. *Cornelius Lampsin*, who had a considerable interest at the court of *France*, procured letters patents from *Lewis* XIV. creating him *Baron* of *Tabago*, which letters patents passed the great seal in the month of *August* 1662, and were registred in the parliament of *Paris* the year following.

lowing. The *Lampsins* procured also a concession from the *Dutch West-India* company, and with the concurrence and consent of the States General sent over Mr. *Hubert de Beveren*, with the title of governor of *Tabago*. This gentleman upon his arrival there, began to put all things upon a new foot. He called the harbour *Lampsin* bay, the town, now much enlarged and decorated with some public buildings, *Lampsinburgh*; he constructed likewise upon an eminence that commanded it a regular fortress called *Lampsinberg*, and another to which he gave the name of *Fort Beveren*, and made it the place of his residence; he likewise added two other forts for the protection of the town and harbour, and projected the building another town, on a convenient neck of land, which it was intended should be called *New Flushing*. Under his administration this *Dutch* settlement began to make a figure, many fine cacao walks were laid out, several indigo works erected, and likewise some sugar mills, so that a regular correspondence was now established, between the inhabitants of *Zealand*, and their countrymen in *Tabago*.

The treaty of *Oliva*, between *Charles* XI. of *Sweden* and *John Casimir* King of *Poland*, having restored the Duke of *Courland* to his liberty and to his dominions, he soon after applied himself to the States General to demand the restitution of *Fort James* and his colony in *Tabago*, but without any success. The Duke thereupon

thereupon addressed himself to our King *Charles* II. for the support of his title; and in consequence of this, that monarch by an instrument bearing date, *November* 17, 1664, granted to *James* Duke of *Courland* and *Semigallia* his heirs and successors, the said island of *Tabago*, in consideration of services therein reserved to the crown of *Great Britain*; and of this concession due notice was given both by the King and by the Duke of *Courland* to the republic. But as at this time, disputes were beginning to arise between the *King* and the *States*, they took very little notice of that grant, and the *Lampsins* on the other hand, sent over repeated orders to their governor and colony, to put every thing there, into the best state of defence possible, foreseeing, as indeed it was not difficult to foresee, that their possessions in that island might be very speedily attacked.

In the first *Dutch* war which quickly followed, we are told by the *French* writers, that the *Dutch* fort in *Tabago* was taken, and the colony reduced by a few *English* privateers, who upon the people's submitting to the *British* crown, suffered them to remain at quiet in their habitations. The same writers say, that after the *French* declared for the *Dutch*, this island was recovered for the latter by the governor of *Grenada*. It is certain it was during the remainder of that war, the rendezvous of the combined fleets of those nations, who from thence did incredible damage, as well to our settlements as commerce;

commerce; and, if their joint fleets had not been defeated, as we have before observed, a little before the close of the war by Sir *John Harman*, who pursued the remains of the *French* to *St. Christophers*, and totally destroyed them there, we should have had very little left in the *West-Indies*. The *Dutch* continued in possession of this isle, in virtue of the general stipulations, but without being expresly mentioned in any article of the treaty of *Breda*. In the space of about five years, which intervened between the first and second *Dutch* war, they fortified this island with incredible diligence, so that at the time it broke out, they looked upon their new town, under the protection of three good forts with a numerous artillery, to be in a manner impregnable. In 1673, however, Sir *Tobias Bridges* plundered the isle, and carried off four hundred prisoners. As we made a seperate peace in the succeeding year with the republic, the *Dutch* in *Tabago* were freed from the apprehensions of our making them any farther visits, which encouraged them to attempt the conquest of the island of *Cayenne* from the *French*, in which they succeeded. But the Count *d'Estrees* Vice Admiral of *France*, being sent with a powerful armament into those parts, recovered *Cayenne* and appeared before *Tabago*; in the port of which lay *James Binkes* Admiral of *Zealand*, with a stout squadron of *Dutch* ships. The Count attacked him on the third of *March*, which was *Good-Friday*, in 1677, both by land and sea, and

after

after a very obstinate engagement, in which he lost his own ship and several others, was forced to retire. The conduct of the Count *d'Estrees*, notwithstanding this repulse as he destroyed the enemies squadron in port, was highly applauded by the *French* court, who sent him thither again with a stronger squadron towards the close of the year. He then landed his forces, invested the principal fort, but finding it strongly fortified, and well provided, he had recourse to a bombardment, and the third bomb that was thrown, falling into a magazine of powder, a great part of the fortress was blown up, in which Admiral *Binkes*, most of the officers, and a great part of the garrison perished. This made the reduction of the colony very easy, and the Count *d'Estrees*, no doubt in consequence of orders he had received at home, utterly destroyed it, *December* 27, 1677, upon which *Lewis* XIV. caused a magnificent medal to be struck, in order to perpetuate the memory of that event.

The *Dutch* being thus entirely dispossessed of *Tabago*, the Duke of *Courland* resumed his design of settling it, for which he appointed one Capt. *Pointz* his agent in *England*, and obtained his *Britannic* Majesty's orders to Sir *Jonathan Atkins*, then our governor of the *Leeward Islands*, to protect his ships and subjects in that enterprize. In 1683 Capt. *Pointz* published here at *London*, proposals at large in the Duke's name, promising great encouragement to any *English* subjects,
who

who were inclined to go thither. It does not however appear, that thefe had any great effect, but it manifeftly proves, that the Duke's title to this ifland, under the grant from the crown of *Great Britain*, was then looked upon as inconteftible. As a ftill farther proof of this, it may not be amifs to obferve, that upon an application made to *Lewis* XIV. by fome of his own fubjects, for a grant of that ifland, under colour of its belonging to the crown of *France* in right of conqueft, it was rejected. The King faying, it belonged to a neutral Prince, from whom he had received no provocations, and to whom he would do no hurt. In 1693, when both we and the *Dutch* were at war with *France*, Mr. *Pointz* republifhed his propofals, under the patronage and protection of King *William*, of which no notice was taken by the ftates.

The male line of the *Houfe of Kettler*, Dukes of *Courland*, extinguifhed in 1737, in the perfon of Duke *Ferdinand*, fon to Duke *James*, to whom the ifland of *Tabago* had been granted, and of courfe upon his demife, the *Fief* returned to the crown of *Great Britain*; in confequence of which, our right thereto was afferted by the governor of *Barbadoes*. The *Dutch* notwithftanding this, fuffered their *Weft-India* company to grant a commiffion of governor of *Tabago* to one of their fubjects; and though the neutrality of the four iflands was ftipulated by the treaty of *Aix-la-Chapelle*, yet the Marquis *de Caylus*, then general of the *French* iflands, declared
roundly

roundly and positively that it belonged to *France*, and actually sent down a force thither to settle and fortify it, notwithstanding the present Admiral, then Captain *Tyrrel*, in his Majesty's ship the *Chesterfield*, was sent by the government of *Barbadoes* to prevent so flagrant an infringement of treaties. On the spirited representation however of his Grace the Duke of *Bedford* then secretary of state, and the application of the late Earl of *Albemarle*, then our ambassador at the court of *Versailles*; the *French* court thought proper to disavow this proceeding, to dispatch a frigate to bring home the Marquis *de Caylus* to answer for his conduct, and to direct that the *island* should be immediately abandoned.

It has ever since remained in this condition without any settled inhabitants, except a very few *Indians*, who live in huts upon the sea coasts towards the north extremity of the island. It is true, both the *English* and *French* turtlers come hither occasionally, remain some time upon the island, and during that space erect huts as a kind of temporary dwellings, till they have supplied themselves with turtle and manatee, and then they return to their respective homes. As to the *Indians* before-mentioned, they are a very quiet, harmless, tractable people, and being well used and treated with indulgence may without question be rendered very serviceable. As enthusiastically fond as they are of liberty, they may be easily made sensible of the advantages derived to them by *British* protection, for being equally

equally afraid, and not without juſt reaſon of the *Indians* in *Dominica* and *St. Vincent*, and of thoſe upon the continent; they cannot but be pleaſed to find themſelves covered from their inſults, and ſure of living in peace and in their own manner. It is true they labour little, becauſe they are not ſenſible of many wants, yet it is not labour of which they are afraid, but of being forced to labour. If therefore they have aſſurances given them, that their freedom ſhall be preſerved, that they ſhall be conſidered as *Britiſh* ſubjects, by having ſtrict and ſpeedy juſtice done them; and, if they have preſents made them of thoſe trifles that they value, and thoſe cheap and common inſtruments which are requiſite for cultivating their land; it may reaſonably be preſumed, that they will quickly become familiar with the firſt ſettlers, and that the younger ſort eſpecially may be wrought upon by gentle uſage and rewards, to do a multitude of little ſervices to the colony, which will ſave time to the white people, and labour to their ſlaves. When they are once uſed to this ſort of employment, come to have a reliſh for gratifications, and by ſeeing our manner of living become ſenſible of their own wants, and with how much caſe they may be ſupplied; they will gradually grow more ſociable, and of courſe be rendered more uſeful.

As this iſland in the ſtate it now is, abounds (as has been already obſerved) with a vaſt variety of different ſorts of timber, all of them
allowed

allowed to be excellent in their respective kinds; it may perhaps deserve some consideration in the first settling it, whether proper officers might not be appointed to secure all the advantages that may be drawn from this circumstance to the public. It is by no means intended, that the first planters should be deprived of the necessary use of all kinds of timber for buildings and utensils, but that this should be cut in a proper method and with discretion, and the rather, because nothing has been more loudly exclaimed against by the sensible men in all the other islands, than the undistinguishing and destructive havock made amongst the woods, without any regard to the general interest, or the least respect paid to that of posterity. By such a method the country may be properly and regularly cleared and opened, and as from the nature of the soil and climate, vegetation is extremely quick, a succession of useful trees may be constantly maintained. By this means, valuable cargoes will be furnished of fine woods for the use of joiners, cabinet-makers, and turners; the necessary materials for dying cloth, silk, and linnen, obtained in the highest perfection, and a vast variety of gums, balsams, and other costly and efficacious medicines may be procured in their genuine and most perfect state. By this precaution very large sums, which we now pay to foreigners will be saved to the nation, the improvement of our manufactures facilitated, and the exportation of these bulky commodities prove a great benefit to our navigation. By putting the direction of these things under the management of capable persons, new lights will continually arise from experience, and new acquisitions may be made of rich and valuable plants from the continent of *South-America*, from *Africa*, and even from the *East-Indies*. The looking after these woods may furnish a proper and easy employment to the *Indians*; in which, if bred to it, their children would certainly delight, and the profits arising from the exportation to *Europe*, might constitute a public revenue for the support of the fortifications and other expences of government, which would be a great ease to the industrious planters, and thereby procure a constant attention in their assemblies, to preserve and promote a design equally serviceable to their mother country and themselves; and considered in this light, it might become a useful precedent in the establishment of something of the like kind in other colonies, and would be attended with no inconveniences whatever.

In the next place we shall take the liberty of observing, that there is at least the highest probability of our being able to produce all the valuable spices of the *East-Indies* in this island. To begin with cinnamon. This is said to grow in some of the other *West-India* islands, and General *Codrington* had once an intention to try how much it might be improved, by a regular cultivation in his island of *Barbuda*. It is universally allowed, that the bark of what is called

the

the wild cinnamon-tree in *Tabago* is beyond comparison, the best in all the *West-Indies*, and even in its present state may be made an article of great value. The bark, when cured with care, differs from that in the *East-Indies*, by being stronger and more acrid while it is fresh, and when it has been kept for some time, it loses that pungency and acquires the flavour of cloves. This is precisely the spice which the *Portuguese* call *Crava de Maranabon*, the *French Canelle Gerofléé*, and the *Italians Canella Garofanata*. There is a very considerable sale of this at *Lisbon*, *Paris*, and over all *Italy*. This kind of spice is drawn chiefly from *Brazil*, and the *Portuguese* believe that their cinnamon-trees were originally brought from *Ceylon* while it was in their possession, but that through the alteration of soil and climate they are degenerated into this kind of spice, and this may very probably be true. However from their size and number it seems to admit of no doubt, that the cinnamon-trees actually growing in *Tabago*, are the natural production of that island, and the point with us is to know what improvements may be made with respect to these.

It may seem a little new, but we hope to render it highly probable, that the sole difference in cinnamon arises from culture. In the first place it is allowed, both by the *Dutch* and *Portuguese*, that there are no less than ten different kinds in the island of *Ceylon*, which is the clearest evidence, that this tree is every where subject to variation from the circumstances of soil and exposition. It is secondly allowed, that even the best finest and first sort of cinnamon-tree does not preserve its high qualites beyond seventeen, eighteen, or at most twenty years. The reason assigned for this by the *Dutch*, is that the *camphire*, as the tree grows older, rises in such quantities as to penetrate the bark; and thereby alter its flavour, which accounts very well for the different taste of the *Brazil* and *Tabago* cinnamon, as the trees must be at least five times more than their proper age. It is thirdly allowed, that the fairest and finest cinnamon grows upon young trees, planted in vallies near the sea side, naturally covered with white sand, where they are perfectly unshaded and exposed to the hottest sun; that at five years old they begin to bark the branches; and, that the tree continues to produce fine-flavoured cinnamon for the number of years already mentioned. They then cut it down to the root, from whence in a year or two it sprouts again, and in five or six they begin to bark the young plants. There is one circumstance more necessary to be observed, the true cinnamon is the inner bark of the branches grown to a proper size, and when taken off and exposed to be dried is of a green colour and has no smell, but as the watry particles are exhaled, and the bark curls in the manner we receive it, the colour changes, and the odour of the cinnamon gradually increases. What then is there to hinder our attempting the cultivation

of

of cinnamon, which nature feems to have produced in as much perfection in *Tabago* as in *Ceylon*?

In the fecond place, we have mentioned that the *nutmeg* as well as the *cinnamon-tree*, is a native of this ifle; and as we likewife obferved, is reported, to be defective and inferior in its kind, to the fame fort of fpice in, or at leaft as it is brought to us from the *Eaft-Indies*. We cannot doubt of the fact, that is, of the nutmeg's growing here; becaufe we find it afferted, in a book addreffed to Mr. *de Beveren* then governor of *Tabago*. A man who had invented a falfehood, would hardly have had the boldnefs to repeat it, not only to a refpectable perfon, but to the perfon in the world, who muft have the cleareft knowledge of its being a falfehood. There is a current tradition in *Guadaloupe*, that one of the *Dutch* fugitives who fled thither from *Brazil*, brought and planted a nutmeg-tree in that ifland, which grew and flourifhed, but before it bore fruit, another *Dutchman*, jealous of the intereft of his country, cut down and deftroyed it. It has fince then been always matter of doubt amongft the *French*; whether this tree grew originally in *Brazil*, or whether the *Dutchman* who planted it, had brought it thither from the *Eaft-Indies*. The latter feems to be the moft probable, fince we have no account of nutmeg-trees growing in *Brazil*. In refpect however to this ifle, we have no occafion to tranfport it either from

*Brazil*, if it was there, or from the *East-Indies*, if it was not. The nutmeg-tree that naturally grows in *Tabago*, is in all probability as true, and may by due care and pains be rendered as valuable a nutmeg as those that grow any where else, for the fact really is, that wherever there are nutmegs, there are wild nutmegs, or as some stile them mountain nutmegs, which are longer and larger, but much inferior in the flavour to the true nutmeg, and are very liable to be worm-eaten; the point is, to know how these defects may be remedied, or in other words, wherein the difference consists, between the wild, tasteless, and useless nutmeg, and that which is true, aromatic, and of course a valuable spice.

The nutmegs which the *Dutch* bring into *Europe*, grow in the islands of *Banda*, which are six in number, but the *Dutch* long ago confined the nutmeg plantations to *three* of them only, and took all the precautions imaginable, to hinder their being cultivated any where else, that they might the better confine the profits arising from this rich spice, to their own company. The true nutmeg, is of the size and height of a pear-tree, the wild or mountain nutmeg is a larger tree, not so well furnished with branches, but the leaves are broader and longer. The nutmegs are planted in *closes* or *parks*, in a regular order, and with much labour and industry are carefully kept free from all weeds or plants that may exhaust their nourishment,

rishment, or to speak more intelligibly are attended with the same diligence as a *Cacao* walk. Besides this, they are defended on the outside, by one or two rows of trees, taller in size, which secure them from sudden gusts of wind and from the sea air, by both of which they would be otherwise prejudiced.

They afford three harvests in the year, the first is towards the latter end of *March* and the beginning of *April*, the product then is but small, consisting only of such as are full ripe or fallen; but then these are the finest, both with respect to the nut and to the mace. The second is the great harvest, in the latter end of *July* and the beginning of *August*, when all are gathered that are ripe. The third is in *November*, and is properly the gleaning, for then they take all that are left upon the tree. When they are thus gathered, they are stripped with a knife of their outer husks, which resemble those of walnuts; the inner coat which is the MACE, is next taken off, with great care and as whole as it is possible, it is then of a bright crimson colour, but when cautiously dried becomes of a yellow brown, thin, brittle, shining, oily, and of a pleasing aromatic fragrance. The nut thus despoiled of both coats is exposed to the sun for a day to dry, and this operation is finished in three or four days more, by exposing them though at a convenient distance to the heat of fire. Then the shell which is thin, and has a very slight pellicle adhering to it, is removed,

removed, and the kernel or nutmeg taken out. This is likewise very carefully dried, and when that is done, the nuts are put by small parcels into wicker baskets, in which they are dipped in a strong solution of lime, made with calcined shells, mixed with sea water. The great secret lies in thus curing of them, by which they are hindered from corrupting, from suffering by the worm, or losing their virtue by the humidity of the sea air when transported to *Europe*.

We may reasonably conclude from this account, that the nutmeg-tree being a delicate plant, owes its high aromatic flavour, to its being industriously cultivated, with great caution, and all this in a proper soil. It must be also observed, that even amongst the trees in the nutmeg parks, there are some that produce long and ill-shaped nuts, with very little flavour, which are stiled *male* nutmegs; whereas the round aromatic fruit, which is brought to *Europe*, is called the *female* nutmeg. The smallest of the nutmeg parks or closes, do not contain above an *English rood* of land, but the largest contain three, four, or five times as much. The whole quantity collected in the three harvests, and in a favourable season, seldom amounts to more than *three hundred* tons of nutmegs, and from *seventy* to *eighty* tons of mace. From this succinct account of the nature and method of cultivating this valuable spice, it will certainly appear that it may be very well worth the trouble and expence of

making

making the experiment, whether by the same method, the wild nutmeg-tree as it is called in *Tabago*, may not be reclaimed and improved, so as gradually to acquire all the virtue and odour of the true spice. There may no doubt many difficulties occur, both in the cultivation and in the curing; but the vigour, the sagacity, the indefatigable diligence of *British* planters, will very probably overcome all these.

It must be acknowledged, that we have no account of, the tree, that produces *cloves*, growing either in this, or in any other island in *America*. It is not however impossible, that when the productions of *Tabago* shall be more attentively examined, by capable persons, we may possibly find, that nature has produced this spice here, as well as the rest. No great weight, indeed no weight at all ought to be laid on this supposition, which is mentioned only, that an enquiry may be made. But if we take it for granted, that the clove does not grow here, we may nevertheless venture to assert, that the nature of the soil and climate considered, together with the size and situation of the isle, the natural production of other spices, and the flavour of cloves, that is said to predominate in these, make it not at all improbable, that if the clove was introduced, it would thrive here. That it may be introduced, and without much difficulty, will appear no unreasonable assertion, when we consider that this plant may be obtained from *Borneo*, *Ceram*, *Mindanao*,

*Mindanao*, and perhaps other places, without the leave of the *Dutch*. They are at present indeed, in the sole possession of the spice trade, and this they owe, as in truth they do most of their advantages, to a very commendable care, indefatigable industry, and constant circumspection. For as on the one hand, they have been at inexpressible pains, in procuring and preserving the perfection of these valuable commodities, by a skilful cultivation; so on the other hand, they have been at little less trouble to extirpate these precious vegetables, where nature had produced them, but where they found it extremely difficult, if not impossible to confine their production solely to their own profit. There seems to be no just cause therefore, why we should not imitate them, as far as it is fit to imitate them, or any political injustice, in rescuing, if we are able to do it, for our own benefit, any of the gifts of nature, that they from the same motive would keep within their own power.

The tree which produces the *clove*, is said to resemble an olive, round in its form, with a smooth glossy bark, rising to the height of six or seven feet, and then throwing out branches which aspire and form at length a kind of a pyramid. The leaves are shaped like those of the laurel, but smaller, of a deep dark green on one side, and of a lighter yellowish green on the other. The pistils of the flower, form what is called *the clove*, which is so well known,

that

that it need not be described, of a lively green colour before it becomes ripe, assuming then a bright crimson hue, and becoming of a dark brown when it is cured. The leaves are produced regularly on the sides of the young twigs, at the extremity of which, the flowers and consequently the cloves hang in clusters. This is a succinct, but it is hoped an intelligible account of this spice, so far as regards our purpose, those who would be more minutely informed, may have recourse to Botanical writers, and particularly to a work lately published in *Holland*, where they may meet with every thing they can desire, and be from thence more effectually convinced, that what has been already asserted, is strictly agreeable to truth.

The *clove* like the *nutmeg-trees*, are planted in small closes, and there cultivated with all possible care and attention. The soil and exposition are chosen with great skill, and all the ground is kept continually clear of weeds, plants, and bushes. Some old writers tell us, that this plant is of so very hot a nature, as to suffer nothing to rise under it, but the real fact is, as we have stated it. There is no other vegetable suffered to grow in the closes destined for the cloves, because this would deprive them of their nutriment, and diminish the strength and perfection of the spice, which though it derives its form and texture from nature, owes much of its delicate fragrance and flavour, as all other spices do, to cultivation and art; and to that

assiduous

assiduous attention, that is employed in the planting, preserving, gathering, and curing them, without which they would not either have gained or maintained that degree of excellence, which has now subsisted for ages.

The harvest of the *cloves*, according to the forwardness or backwardness of the season, is in the middle of the month of *October*, through the whole of *November*, and even to the middle of *December*. The common notion that they are shaken down from the tree, is absolutely false, and they are on the contrary gathered with much attention and precaution. They climb up the tree, and collect with their hands the bunches, as far as they are within reach, and lay them in baskets. In order to come at the rest, they use long canes with a little hook at the end, with which they beat down the clusters, but with all possible tenderness, that they may avoid breaking the extremity of the twigs, by which the tree would be much injured. When the cloves are thus collected in baskets, they are dried with the same caution that is used in regard to nutmegs, and after they are thus cured, they are like the nutmegs carefully sorted. Such as are quite green, and such as are come to their full crimson colour are rejected, for both would spoil in their passage. Those, and only those that are in proper order, are packed with the greatest care, and carried to the company's magazines, till such time as they are either sold, or embarked for *Batavia*. Every method

method possible is devised and practised, to prevent private or fraudulent trade, for which their prosecutions are as strict, as their penalties are severe; and yet there are cases in which both prove ineffectual. The natives sometimes find ways and means to convey them into the neighbouring islands, where though with great secrecy, they are sold to other *European* traders. Neither is it without example, that some of the company's servants have adventured, dangerous as it is, upon this illicit traffic, the amount of which after all, is not very considerable.

The harvest is annual, notwithstanding that some writers tell us, it happens but once in eight years. They are sometimes very plentiful, and at others very sparing, according as the monsoon sets in wet or dry. In the best years, they may produce about two thousand bahars, which is about *five hundred* and *fifty* ton. In a very bad year, not half so much, but as the magazines are always kept well supplied, there comes usually the same quantity to the *Europe* market, where at the *Dutch* sales, and indeed over all *India*, the price of spice very rarely alters. The *clove* retains its vigour, longer than either the *cinnamon* or the *nutmeg*, for it continues to bear plentifully, in a good season, for fifty or sixty years, and in the *Moluccas* they did not reckon a tree old, in less than a hundred. The number of bearing trees, in all the closes, are computed at *two hundred and fifty thousand*, exclusive of the young plants, that are intended to replace the old trees when they are become paſt bearing.

This point has been dwelt upon, becauſe of its extraordinary importance, though it is not entirely new, for the thought of raiſing the ſpices of the *Eaſt* in the *Weſt-Indies*, occurred as has been already hinted to us and to the *French* long ago, though it never was attempted, or indeed could be attempted with ſo fair a proſpect of ſucceſs, as in this iſland. But it muſt not be diſſembled, that fair and flattering as the appearance may be, the project lies open to ſome plauſible objections; the moſt material of which, we will ſtate fairly, and then endeavour to anſwer them fully and freely. This we rather incline to do, that it may appear this propoſal has been duly weighed and maturely examined, before it was offered to the inſpection of the public, and this purely for its own advantage; and that the profits of our new acquiſitions, may be rendered not only advantageous, but as ſpeedily advantageous, and advantageous in as many different methods, as it is poſſible. For we cannot contrive too many, or too ſudden means of reimburſing, more eſpecially by the help of our new plantations, that large expence of treaſure, which the nation has been at in ſupport of the old, for this is the beſt way of juſtifying that meaſure, as well as of preventing the neceſſity of our being put to the like expences again.

The

The first objection is, *that though* Tabago *lie farther south, or rather nearer to the* Line *than any of our islands, yet it does not lie so far south, or so near the* Line, *as any of the countries that produce any of these spices.* At first sight this must be allowed to carry a great shew of reason, but when strictly and candidly examined, it will not appear very formidable. In the first place, this assertion takes for granted more than we know, or at least more than we know with any certainty; for though the objection be truly stated, with respect to the places from whence most of the spices are known to come, yet, who will venture to affirm, that they do not grow in any part of the *East*, above ten degrees from the *Line?* But even supposing this true, with respect to the *East Indies*, it is contrary to fact, with regard to the *West*, since cinnamon and nutmegs have been found in *Tabago*; and, according to the *French* tradition in *Guadaloupe*. If this weaken the objection, it will be still much more weakened, if we consider what has been already proved from the evidence of facts, that the principal qualities of spices, are not so much owing to climate and soil, as they are to care and cultivation. We have two of the three spices actually in *Tabago*, so that if the expression may be allowed, *nature* has done *her* part, she has done all that she ever does, she has brought forth the *children*, and now calls upon *art* and *industry* to afford them, if we may so speak, a proper *education*. In order to encourage

rage us to undertake it; let us consider, that *ginger, sugar, indigo,* and many other things might be mentioned, which are now common to *both* of the *Indies,* chiefly thro' the care and pains that have been bestowed upon them; and, therefore, if the same means are employed, why may not the same effects follow, with respect to *spices?* If this objection had any real weight, it had stopped our attempts long ago, but if experience in some cases shews us, that it has really no weight at all, why should we conclude in its favour against others? If interest was strong enough to get the better of indolence and prejudice in respect to those commodities, why should not a superior interest induce us to make still greater efforts, in respect to commodities of still greater value?

The second great objection is, *that this proposition grasps* too much; *that* nature, *or rather* providence *has diffused its* blessings *through* different *climates and countries; that particularly in regard to* spices, CINNAMON *flourishes in* Ceylon, CLOVES *in the* Moluccas, NUTMEGS *in the* Isles *of* Banda; *and that possibly* experience *may teach us, that it is beyond the* power, *and consequently not to be reached by the* contrivance *of* men *to alter her* laws, *and to monopolize her* benefits. This like the former, assumes what should have been first incontestibly proved; and takes for its foundation, a supposition instead of a fact. For though it be true, that cinnamon, nutmegs, and cloves, are, and always have been, brought

to

to us from different places, yet there is no ground to conclude from thence, that this proceeds from a law of nature; or that providence never designed they should be produced any where else. If we may give credit to authors of great authority, and even to some who have been eye-witnesses; all these three kinds of spices, are actually to be found growing in the island of *Borneo*. Two of them, are said to be produced in the highest perfection, in the island of *Mindanao*, which is one of the *Phillipines*. Besides, though cloves grow naturally in the *Moluca Islands*, and were first brought from thence into *Europe* by the *Portuguese*, which produced the discovery of the new course to the *East-Indies*, by the streights of *Magellan*, from the desire which the *Spaniards* had, to share in that rich trade; yet, since the *Dutch* have dispossessed both those nations, they have found it for their interest, without respecting this supposed law of nature, not only to remove them, but to extirpate them from those islands, and have planted them in *Amboyna*, where they grow perfectly well, and where probably they never had grown, if not carried thither in this manner. Upon the same principle, they restrained the nutmegs which grew in all the six islands of *Banda*, to three; and which is still more to the purpose, they began more than forty years ago, and perhaps have by this time compleated, the removing the nutmegs into *Amboyna*. It is indeed true, that they did not succeed at first in this attempt,

attempt; upon which it was furmized, that the same soil might not be proper for both kinds of spices. However, the *Dutch* spirit of perseverance was not to be moved by this suggestion. They judged there might be other causes for this miscarriage; which having traced out and removed, nutmegs and cloves have been ever since cultivated with the like ease, and with the like success in *Amboyna*. As they were, and still are, entirely masters of the cinnamon trade in *Ceylon*, and could have no rational prospect of being as much masters of it, if they had attempted the cultivation of that spice any where else, they have very prudently left it where it was. Thus by a brief discussion of this objection, the reader has before him, new, stronger, and more conclusive reasons than were offered before, in favour of our attempting to meliorate the two kinds of spices that are there already, and to introduce the third into our island of *Tabago*.

A third objection is, *that even supposing this scheme* practicable, *it seems to be too extensive for the small island of* Tabago; *and therefore more perhaps might possibly be obtained, by aiming at less.* In answer to this, we must observe, that if the first and general position be right, that the excellence of all kinds of spices depends chiefly upon cultivation, in a proper soil and climate; it will then follow, that small as the island of *Tabago* is, there will be found in it much more land, than is sufficient to answer all the purposes,

poses that we have mentioned. It is indeed true, that the island of *Amboyna* is larger than that of *Tabago*, but then it is a very small part only of that island, which is occupied by the *parks* for cloves and nutmegs; and besides the *Dutch* inhabitants, there are fifty or sixty thousand of the natives, who are subject indeed to them, but who draw their subsistence from other productions of the earth and sea, and not from the spices. This in a smaller degree might be the case in *Tabago*; for though, without doubt, there might be considerable tracts therein, which in point of soil and exposition, may be fit for cinnamon and cloves, yet there may be other, and those too much larger tracts, unfit for that purpose; and which consequently may be applied to cotton, cacao, sugar, or other commodities, which we are equally certain may be raised therein, and which may turn to a very considerable, though possibly the quantity of ground and number of hands considered, not to so large an amount. In respect to cloves, if the island of *Little Tabago*, either derives from nature, or can by industry and art be furnished with a soil, fit to produce them; there is much more room even in that small place, than the *Dutch* employ for that purpose, including the habitations of the slaves, that are destined to their cultivation; the number of which by the way, is under three thousand, and it must be a long time with all our care, before we shall have need of so many. But the principal reason

son of propounding so extensive a scheme is, that the time, the pains, and the expence, that would be required to make the experiment with regard to any one spice, will be very little increased, by attempting them all; and then, if the former objection should be really found to have any weight, we shall be able to discover which of these spices may be cultivated to a high degree of perfection there, and perhaps this can be discovered no other way. Add to this, that *Tabago* is as large as any of the islands till now in our possession, *Jamacia* only excepted; and yet in every one of these islands, we raise several different productions, without any inconvenience, and those who are the best judges, have thought, that even in them, there is still room for introducing more.

In this, if in any of our islands, a free port may be opened, with as many apparent advantages, and perhaps with fewer inconveniences than any where else. For here there is great choice of ports on both sides the island, some, that are by nature very secure, and others that may be made so, at a very small expence. The fertility of the island also is such, as that with benefit instead of prejudice to themselves, the inhabitants will always have it in their power, to relieve the wants of those on board ships, resorting thither for a supply of fresh provisions. Here, in one or more Settlements, spacious magazines might be erected, for the reception of *East-India*, *European*, and *North-America*

*America* commodities; all of which would not fail of finding a vent, and thereby producing an advantageous circulation of commerce and of money. The situation of this island is another great advantage, whether we consider its nearness to the *Spanish* main, or its convenient distance from some other islands, both of which ought to be regarded, in the choice of a free port. It might be also peculiarly advantageous, upon the first settling of the island, as by the hopes of immediate profit, it might attract people, create an instantaneous intercourse, and thereby a lucrative commerce with different parts of the world, which must otherwise prove a work of time. It might also open to us a correspondence with the free *Indians*, who live upon the continent, who would be glad of having access to a country so near them, to which they might go, and from which they might return at pleasure, without danger to their liberty. On the other hand our people would be attentive enough to their own interest; and tho' at first they might find it expedient to make them presents of such things as they saw most pleasing to them, yet in a little time they would make them sensible, that in order to obtain a continuance of such supplies they must be content to render themselves useful in return, either by finding goods to barter, or by undertaking themselves some easy kind of labour, which propositions, if made with address, and prosecuted with humanity and justice, would not fail of making an impression upon them in time; and thereby open the means of having at least some kind of cultivation carried on there by freemen, which would be an acquisition of people, as well as of country. An acquisition not at all the more impracticable, because that hitherto it has never been made. Our planters when they first went to the *West-Indies*, had as little idea of *Negro* slaves, as they have now of *Indians*. In time they may profit as much by the one as by the other.

This point has been very cautiously spoken to, because some not without reason have doubted, whether it might be expedient for us to follow the example of our neighbours in the opening as they have done free ports in *America*. It is indeed certain, that the *Dutch* are very great gainers by those of *Eustatia* and *Caracao*. But there is undoubtedly a very great difference between the maxims of their policy and ours; and therefore there is no drawing any consequence from the success they have met with, to justify our taking the same measure. The *Dutch* are gainers by their commerce, we by our plantations. They thrive by the labour of other nations, we are become rich and potent, by the industry of our own. In a word, the commerce of their islands has promoted their colonies, whereas the produce of our colonies, has been the great support of their commerce. But possibly if we should succeed in raising spices, and make other improvements

ments in this island, hitherto unintroduced into any other; the trade of a free port therein may become very beneficial to its Inhabitants, without any detriment to the mother country. On the contrary great cargoes exported from hence, may be difpofed of there, and produce fuitable returns. At all events, a free port in this ifland might be eafily put, and as eafily kept, under proper regulations, by which the experiment, which is of very great importance, might be effectually made. If when it is made, the inconveniences fhould be found to out-weigh the advantages, or any unforefeen mifchief fhould from thence arife, either to the trade of the other colonies, or that of *Great Britain*; fuch a port might be with facility fuppreffed.

We are now come to the two laft iflands, the value and importance of which we undertook to difcufs, *viz. St. Lucia* and *Granada* with its *dependancies*; the former of thefe being left to *France* by the late definitive treaty, by which alfo the latter is ceded to us. The firft of thefe is called by the *Spaniards*, who difcovered it and impofed this name, *Santa Luzia*; by the *French* ufually ftiled *Aloufie*; and by us *St. Lucia*. It is fituated, twenty-four leagues weft north weft from *Barbadoes*; eight leagues fouth from *Martinico*; fomething more then feven leagues, north by eaft from *St. Vincent*; twenty-feven leagues, fouth from *Dominica*; feventy leagues, fouth eaft from *St. Chriftophers*; forty-five, north weft from *Tabago*, and about thirty-five, north east from *Granada*. The reader sees thus, in one view, how it is disposed, as well with respect to our own as to the *French* islands, upon which its importance is justly supposed to depend.

According to the best accounts we have, and particularly that of Captain *Uring*, who was very attentive in his examination of this country, it is twenty-two *English* miles in length, eleven in breadth, and somewhat more than twenty leagues in circumference. It appears, therefore, to be in point of size, somewhat larger than our island of *St. Vincent*; but is inferior in that respect to *Dominica* and to *Granada*. In regard to climate, there is some variation, in the sentiments of those authors who have mentioned it. There are *French* writers, who say, that the heat being tempered by the breeze from the sea, renders it equally wholesome and pleasant; but there are others, who assert that it is sultry and moist, which renders it far from being healthy. Captain *Uring*, who landed a considerable number of men here, agrees with the former, and commends it highly; but then even he also acknowledges, that in a fortnight's time, his people grew so weak and sickly, as to put it absolutely out of his power to defend himself against the *French*, even if they had not invaded the island, as they did, with great superiority of numbers. It is also owned by him, as well as by all the *French* writers, that it is as much, or more infested with venomous serpents

than

than *Martinico*, and it may not be improper to remark, that except in thefe two iflands, and in that of *Bekia*, which now belongs to us, there are none of thefe dangerous reptiles, for the fnakes, though long and large in feveral of the other iflands, are by no means dangerous.

The appearance of this ifland is rugged and mountainous, towards the fouth-weft extremity, there are two high fugar-loaf hills, called by the *French, Les Pitons de Aloufie*, by which the ifland is eafily known. They are very fteep, and the air on their fummits is faid to be very cold. There runs alfo a long range of mountains, fome of which are of a great height, along the windward fide of the ifland; but at the bottom of thefe, there is a fine plain, near fifteen miles long, and between two and three broad; the foil of which is very rich and fruitful. There are befides thofe already mentioned, feveral other mountains, with pleafant vallies between them. The foil in general, is much of the fame nature, and held to be very little, if at all, inferior to that of *Martinico*; fo that there is no doubt if it was equally cultivated, it would yield extraordinary profit, more efpecially, when the country is effectually cleared, which, a few fpots excepted near the fea coaft, is at prefent over-grown with wood. The *French* have a tradition, which however is generally believed, that there is a very rich filver mine upon this ifland, which fome even of the inhabitants of our ifles think has a foundation

in

in truth, and others apprehend to have been thrown out on political motives.

There are very few iflands in *America*, better watered in all refpects than this. Many rivulets run from the mountains into the fea on both fides, and in all of them, there is plenty of different kinds of fifh. It is true, that fome of thefe rivulets, and the fame might be alledged of thofe in other iflands, may be rather ftiled torrents; becaufe, though at fome feafons, they are rapid and full of water; yet in the heat of fummer they are frequently dried up, which is however (as we have obferved) an inconvenience not at all peculiar to *St. Lucia*. There are others that take a ferpentine courfe through the meadows, and render them very luxurious. Springs of frefh water are common almoft every where, and towards the north-weft end of the ifland, there is a large pond or fmall lake. In fome of the vallies, the country is marfhy; but, if once fully inhabited, thefe might be eafily drained, which would add to the falubrity of the air.

The produce of this ifland in its prefent condition, is chiefly timber of all forts, in vaft plenty, and in great perfection. There are likewife all kinds of ground provifions, raifed wherever there are people. The country likewife abounds with wild hogs, with fowl of all kinds, tame as well as wild; a vaft variety of different forts of fifh, and of thefe alfo there are furprizing quantities taken upon the coaft. The *French* many years ago reforted thither chiefly on that account; they
then

then fell to cutting of timber, for the use of the inhabitants of *Martinico*; after this they began to build boats, barks, and at length ships, inviting and encouraging *English* and *Dutch* carpenters to come thither for that purpose; for in those times there were no regular settlers, but the *French* from *Martinico*, sent hither occasionally such sort of people as were troublesome in that colony, and unwilling to bear the restraint of laws. These when they had finished the work for which they came, returned again, and only a few *Indians* and free *Negroes*, with such criminals and bankrupts as were desirous of keeping out of the reach of justice, continued thereon. But by degrees a better sort of people chose to try their fortunes there, began to clear considerable spots of ground, on which they gradually raised very profitable plantations. The chief commodities they raised, were cacao, cotton, and indigo, in which they were very succesful. This naturally increased their numbers, and the trade between *St. Lucia* and *Martinico*, has been for many years, though now and then interrupted, of very great value, though they studied to conceal it as much as possible, for reasons that will hereafter appear.

We come now to treat of the history of this island, as we have done of the rest, and to say the truth, it is more interesting than any of them. It was discovered by the Admiral *Columbus*, on the 13th of *December*, which is the feast-day of this Saint in the *Roman* Calendar, from whom on that account it received her name, but it does not appear that the *Spaniards* ever thought it farther worth their notice; but on the contrary left it as they found it, in the hands of the *Indians*. It was visited by the Earl of *Cumberland*, in 1593; and when this nation was very intent in settling colonies in *Guiana*, a ship dispatched thither, by Sir *Olyff Leigh*, debarked through want of provisions, Captain *Nicholas St. John*, and sixty-six other persons upon this island, where they happened to touch, with a view to their settlement upon it. They were at first well received and kindly treated by the natives, who were then very numerous; and on the other hand, they were very desirous of conciliating their friendship, as they found them possessed of great quantities of valuable goods, which they had taken out of a *Spanish* wreck, and which they bought of them, for knives, hatchets, and other things of small value. It was not long, however, before the *Indians* treacherously endeavoured to surprize them, and by their great superiority in numbers, destroyed the greatest part of them, and the rest escaped with great difficulty, and even of these some few only returned to *England*. This gave a sufficient knowledge of the island, and very probably induced a desire of settling it, as we had undoubtedly a right to chastize those *Indians*, who uninjured and unprovoked had treated our countrymen with so much injustice and barbarity.

This

This inclination clearly appears, by Sir *Thomas Warner*'s sending hither, so early as the year 1626, a small number of people, under the direction of one Mr. *Judge*, who was the first *English* governor in *St. Lucia*. Upon his taking possession of it, we find this isle was inserted, among the other islands, in the Earl of *Carlisle*'s patent, under whose authority, various grants were made, and several supplies of people were sent, not only from the island of *Barbadoes*, but also from the *Bermudas Islands*. There is however no need of insisting particularly on these points, since the *French* writers themselves admit, that we were fully and solely masters therein, in the year 1639. At this time, an unhappy quarrel arose with the *Indians*, who were then very numerous in *Dominica*, and who it seems were cunning as well as strong enough to surprize the *English* inhabitants in *St. Lucia*, and to massacre them as they did without mercy. There was, however, a suspicion in our people, that the *Indians* were incited to, if not assisted in this act, by Mr. *Parquet* the *French* governor of *Martinique*, from which imputation however he justified himself, not by a bare denial of the fact, but by a positive assertion, that he gave them timely notice of it, and advised them to be upon their guard. However this matter might be, the *French* found their title, upon our abandoning the island at this time, and on this pretence, for it certainly merits no better name, Mr. *Parquet* sent over

a small

a small detachment of men to take possession of it, as they actually did, and built a strong house or fort for their own security; and at the same time by the advice of Mr. *Parquet*, who acquired this isle from the *French* company, as his property, and for its security, entered into very close engagements with the *Indians*, to whom he plainly stood indebted for the opportunity of coming into possession of this island.

The name of this *French* governor, thus sent by Mr. *Parquet*, was the Sieur *de Rousselan*; and the reason which determined that shrewd man to make choice of him, was that he had married an *Indian* woman, which made him very acceptable to the savages, with whom he lived with great familiarity, but however from his perfect knowledge of them with due caution. In 1643, our people made a descent upon the island, in order to recover their right, but unfortunately without effect. The two next *French* governors, by trusting them too much, were destroyed by the *Savages*; against the fourth the colony rebelled, and in the time of Mr. *de Aigremont*, in the year 1657, we made another attempt, in which we had again the misfortune to miscarry. Father *Labat* taking no notice of the former, triumphs upon this, and tells us that we were a little of the latest, in letting slip almost twenty years before we renewed our claim; and adds, that during that space, we had taken no precaution to justify our right in *Europe*; without ever reflecting, that during this period,
there

there was no settled or legal government in *England*, which was the true source of this, as well as it also was of many other misfortunes.

King *Charles* II. after the restoration, having appointed *Francis*, Lord *Willoughby* of *Parham*, governor of *Barbadoes* and the *Leeward Islands*, with instructions to vindicate the rights of the crown of *Great Britain* in respect to its possessions in those parts; that noble Peer in 1663, wisely came to an agreement with the *Indians*, and procured from them an authentic cession of their rights to this island; upon which he sent over the next year, colonel *Carew* with a compleat regiment, accompanied by a body of *Indians*, who gave him upon the spot, and in the sight of the *French*, possession of *St. Lucia*, which he occupied and governed by a commission from Lord *Willoughby*, after sending the greatest part of the *French* home to *Martinico*. The next year, there was a farther reinforcement sent, and one Mr. *Cook* was appointed lieutenant governor, who expelled the remainder of the *French* and demolished their fort. The *French* writers observe truly, that this was done in a time of full peace; and, therefore, if it had not been the retaking possession of a country, to which we had an ancient and a just claim, this must have been, and no doubt would have been considered, as an act of hostility, by *Lewis* XIV. and that it was not so considered, is as clear a negative proof as can be brought of the validity of our title. There is

no

no mention made of this island, in the treaty of *Breda*, becaufe then it was in our poffeffion; though the colony might be weak and infignificant, but, if at this time the *French* had any notions of their having a juft right, there is no doubt, they would have afferted it, more efpecially after what had happened.

It was henceforward always included in the governor of *Barbadoes*' commiffion, and he was inftructed to maintain our right, to hinder the *French* from fettling or trading thither, from cutting wood, or from doing any other act, that might impeach our fovereignty, which our governors performed, fome with more, fome with lefs punctuality. Sir *Edwyn Stede*, then colonel *Stede*, and lieutenant general of *Barbadoes*, in the reign of King *James* II. fent captain *Temple* thither, who removed all the *French* that could be found, fent them to *Martinico*, and fignified his proceedings to the count *de Blenac*, general of the *French* iflands, requiring him not to fuffer any within his government, to plant, fifh, hunt, or cut wood on that ifland, without licence firft obtained from the governor of *Barbadoes*. It is indeed true, that the *French* ambaffador complained of this by a memorial, which did not hinder captain *Temple* from being fent thither again for the like purpofes, and an *Englifh* frigate with a fleet from *Barbadoes*, was actually riding in one of the harbours of *St. Lucia*, when the treaty of neutrality was figned at *London*; of which treaty, as foon as colonel *Stede*

*Stede* had notice, he caused it to be solemnly proclaimed by his authority in *St. Lucia*, as in an island dependant upon his government. After the revolution, and after the treaty of *Ryswic*, in *June* 1699, Colonel *Gray*, governor of *Barbadoes*, asserted the right of the crown of *Great Britain*, by sending away some *French* who had brought *Negroes*, and were actually beginning to plant there. Things remained in this situation, down to the treaty of *Utrecht*, in which it was certainly a great omission, that our right to this, and the rest of the islands was not fully and clearly established, as it easily might have been, but notwithstanding this neglect, that right was no way injured, by the absolute silence of that treaty upon this subject.

However the *French* becoming more and more desirous, in consequence of their increasing abilities, to settle this island, the Regent Duke of *Orleans* was prevailed upon in the month of *August* 1718, to make an absolute grant of this island to the Marshal *d'Estrées*, reserving only faith and homage to the crown of *France*; and which may, perhaps, give some light into at least one principal motive of obtaining this grant, the *tenth* of the clear profits of any mine or mines, which should be wrought by the marshal or his assignees. This awakened our court, who thereupon expostulated with that of *Versailles*, in such terms, as induced the regent to consent, to the immediate evacuation of the island; for which purpose an order was sent to the Governor-General of the *French* iſlands, to ſee this evacuation punctually executed, and the Marſhal *d'Eſtrées* likewiſe ſurrendered his grant. His late Majeſty King *George* I. in 1722, made a grant of this and the iſland of *St. Vincent*, to His late Grace of *Montagu*, who, like a generous and public ſpirited nobleman, made a large and very expenſive armament in order to take poſſeſſion of thoſe iſlands, and ſent Captain *Uring* as his governor to *St. Lucia*. We have already mentioned, that the *French* in the beginning of the ſucceeding year, obliged that gentleman by a very ſuperior force, to abandon that deſign; and, if our deſiſting upon this occaſion, from a title which to be ſure was well conſidered before that grant was made, was to ſhew that we were as capable of condeſcenſion as the *French* court had been in the caſe of Marſhal *d'Eſtrées*; it muſt be allowed one of the beſt excuſes that could be made for ſuch a proceeding, though in reality it ſhould ſeem that, when the thing came to the point, it was not thought expedient by either court, to hazard a war for the chance of obtaining this iſland.

Things reſted again in this indeterminate ſtate, for near ſeven years, when under colour of wooding and watering, which was permitted on both ſides, the ſubjects of the two crowns, began to fix themſelves in that iſland, without any of their former animoſity, and gradually entered into an amicable correſpondence, which produced a ſort of commerce, that gave umbrage to
the

the government in the *French* islands, and upon complaints made from thence to the court of *Versailles*, representations in regard to that illicit commerce, were made here. These produced, in 1730, an agreement between both courts, to cause that island to be effectually evacuated and abandoned both by the *English* and the *French*, and this was said to be carried into execution in 1733. Yet, if any credit be due to the most solemn assertions of the inhabitants of our *Leeward Islands*, this evacuation, tho' real on the part of the *English*, was illusory only on the side of the *French*, who shut up their houses indeed, and carried away their *Negroes* in obedience to the *French* King's proclamation, but returned to them again in the space of a few days, and not only continued to occupy, but to extend them. This was not the case of our subjects, who had made small settlements there; for they fairly abandoned what little spots they had settled, and brought away their *Negroes* and stock. But in process of time, both they and other planters revived their trade with the *French*, which induced the court of *Versailles* to sollicit another evacuation in 1740, when Capt. *Hawke* (now Sir *Edward*) was sent by Mr. *Byng*, at that time his Majesty's governor of *Barbadoes*, to see it effectually performed on both sides; previous to this however, that prudent as well as gallant officer, thought proper to erect a post, and upon it to display the *British* flag, that this might not be construed into relinquishing our right to that island; upon which the Sieur *de Viellecourt*, a *French* officer, set up a *white* flag with the like intention. The war breaking out soon after, things remained in this state, till the conclusion of the peace of *Aix-la-Chapelle*, in *October* 1748; in consequence of which, it was again stipulated, that both parties should evacuate; which, however, was not better observed by the *French* than before. In pursuance also of that treaty, the discussing the rights of both crowns was committed to commissaries, and the papers drawn up by them are in the hands of the public. By the late definitive treaty, our right is confessed by the *French*, since they would not have accepted from us, what they thought we had no title to give; and thus after a contest of more than a century, the *French* are at last by the cession of our *right* left in *possession* of this island.

It must be allowed, that the *British* nation had long entertained an earnest desire of adding *St. Lucia* to the rest of her possessions in the *West-Indies*, for which some just, and many plausible reasons were given; at the time more especially, when the late Duke of *Montagu* obtained his grant. It was then alledged, that the island was wonderfully fertile, that it abounded in timber, which was much wanted in our islands; that it was excellently watered, had many convenient bays, and at least one very fine port. The object then principally in view, was the planting of *cacao*; and it was asserted that

that this island would produce enough of that commodity to furnish all *Europe*. But since that period, when sugar bore but a low price; our planters were desirous of having it, in order to introduce canes. All these considerations respected its value; but there were besides these some other, from which it was held to be of still greater importance. It was judged an advantageous thing, to interpose one of our own, between *Barbadoes* and the *French* islands; it was thought from the known advantages of its bays and ports to be very commodious for our squadrons, and it was believed that it might in many respects, prove a great check upon the *French*. It lay to the windward of *Martinico*, and so near it, that nothing could be done there, without our having immediate intelligence. Descents upon that, and upon the rest of the *French* islands might have been faciliated thereby, and all their naval operations must have been embarrassed at least, if not totally frustrated, if we were once masters of that isle. All these ideas, being placed in the strongest point of light, heightened by the most advantageous representations, and no-body undertaking, what indeed would have been thought an invidious task, to call them to a critical examination, a general opinion from thence prevailed, that among the *Neutral* islands, there was not one comparable to *St. Lucia*.

Some objections, however, have been since started, and those too of a nature, that may possibly render them worthy of our notice. We now know from experience, that the country is very far from being healthy. It is so full of venomous creatures of different sizes, that the *French* settled there, were never able to stir abroad but in boots. It is not only very mountainous, but even the flat country is full of marshes. It lies so immediately within the view, and under the power of the well-settled colony of *Martinico*, that without being at a great expence in fortifications, and keeping a constant military force there for its defence, we could scarce hope, that it would ever have been thoroughly settled. If even with the assistance of fortifications and a regular force, it had been settled, it might have been found impracticable to secure it, as there are so many landing places in different parts of the island; and as in case of a war, this small settlement would have been immediately exposed to the whole strength of the *French* islands, so that the inhabitants might have been ruined, before any assistance could have been sent them; and this, if the country had been recovered, or even quitted by the enemy, would certainly have discouraged our people from settling it again. As the case now stands, the *French* are liable to all these inconveniences; and whoever considers the situation of this island, and of those belonging to us in its neighbourhood, and reflects at the same time, on the superiority of our maritime force, will see, that in time of war, it must be a very precarious possession; more especially, if so

thoroughly

thoroughly settled, as to make the conquest of it a matter of much consequence to us.

The *French* have had their prejudices and prepossessions also in favour of this island, and that in a degree, perhaps superior to our own. In the propositions for a peace, made by the court of *France*, *July* 15, 1761, they proposed that all the *four* islands should still remain neuter, or that *Dominica* and *St. Vincent* being left to the *Indians*, *Tabago* should be left in sovereignty to us, and *St. Lucia* to them; reserving the right any other power might have. This in effect was giving us nothing. They would have kept *St. Lucia* absolutely, have possessed themselves gradually, as has been already explained of *Dominica* and *St. Vincent*, and have set up at a proper time, the claim of the crown of *Spain* to the island of *Tabago*. In the definitive propositions made by Mr. *Stanley*, an offer was made, notwithstanding our being at that time in possession of the island of *Dominica*, to divide the neutral islands, and this was renewed in the *Ultimatum* of the first of *September*, and in the last memoir of the *French*, dated on the ninth of the the same month; this partition was accepted, provided that the island of *St. Lucia* was in that division, left to *France*, and in this state things stood, when the rupture happened of that negotiation. The reason the *French* gave for insisting so peremptorily upon having this island, was that if they had it not, *Martinico* could not be secure. The *French* have a sea phrase,

phrase, *Mettre sous boucle, ou à la boucle.* By this they mean, to put a person or a place into safe custody, or as they explain it in their own language, *Mettre, ou, tenir sous clef; ou, en prison;* that is, to hold under lock and key, or in prison; and in this sense they said that *St. Lucia,* or as they call it, *Aloufie* was the *boucle* of *Martinique,* that is, the latter was shut in and covered by the former. But very probably, they might have other reasons. They certainly know the value of that island better than we. They draw from it timber and provisions, for their other islands; they have a strong persuasion that there is a rich silver mine in it; and it is not impossible, that a great family in *France,* may at a proper time resume their pretensions; and in consequence of them, may flatter themselves with the hopes of drawing a considerable revenue, for concessions or grants of land, from those, who shall settle and cultivate that island.

But sure they were strangely occupied with the notion of *St. Lucia,* not to discern that we possess in *Dominica,* much more than we could possibly have had, if we had kept *St. Lucia.* For *Dominica* lies in the very middle of the channel, between *Martinico* and *Guadaloupe;* to windward of the last of these islands, and not so much to leeward of the former, but that vessels can easily fetch the road of *St. Peter,* which is its principal town and port from *Dominica.* We have in that island also, to leeward

Prince *Rupert*'s bay, and to windward, the *Great* bay; so that having *Barbadoes* to the windward of all, and *Antigua* to leeward of *Guadaloupe*, it is impossible in time of war, that either trade or supplies should get into those *French* islands. A great deal more might be, with equal truth, said upon this subject, but what has been already said is surely sufficient to shew, that to use the *French* phrase, *Dominica* is the *boucle*, not of *Martinico* only, but also of *Guadaloupe*. We have before remarked, that *Dominica* is an island of large extent, very fertile, and of great natural strength; and being once effectually settled, which ought to be, and no doubt will be our first care, may be defended against any force whatever. Whereas *St. Lucia* is so accessible on every side, that it must of necessity fall to a superior maritime force. It was in this sense that we suggested, that the want of ports, with which *Dominica* is reproached, is, its situation in the midst of all the *French* islands considered, so far from being a defect, that it is in reality a convenience; for two ports may be easily fortified and defended; whereas it would be endless, to attempt the securing twenty. It may however be surmized, that in the present circumstances of things, we may have a partiality in favour of an island, that is now become OURS. But this objection we will remove, by producing an authority superior to suspicion or contradiction.

It

It is that of father *Labat*, who was not only a very intelligent person, an inquisitive and strict observer, and an eye-witness of all he wrote, but also an engineer, and in that capacity relied on, for fortifying several places in the *French* islands, in the first year of the current century.

This ingenious person, after giving us an account of *Dominica*, which he very carefully examined; and according to the laudable custom of the *French*, in respect to all places not in their possession, having done his utmost to put it in as low and depreciating a light as possible; proceeds thus, " Though after all, this is an
" isle of very little importance; the *English*
" have notwithstanding made many attempts to
" establish themselves therein, founded upon
" certain pretensions which the *French* have
" always opposed, not only because they were
" in themselves void of any reasonable foun-
" dation, but the rather, because if this island
" should be once in their hands, it would serve
" to cut off the communication between *Marti-*
" *nico* and *Guadaloupe*, in a time of war, and
" reduce the inhabitants of both isles to the last
" extremity."

In our last negotiation with the *French*, they found themselves obliged to give up all pretensions to the *Neutral* islands; but retaining still an obstinate fondness for *St. Lucia*, they had no other way of obtaining it, but by giving us an equivalent. In doing this, both they and we considered it might be rendered a sugar island,

that

that it abounded with valuable timber, and that it had good ports. To balance thefe advantages, they offered us the ifland of *Granada*, and all the iflands dependant upon it, which was accepted. The determining whether this was in every one of thefe refpects a full equivalent, for our ceding *St. Lucia* to them, is the point that is to finifh our enquiry.

The large and noble ifland of *Granada*, lies fouth-weft from *St. Vincent*, feventeen or eighteen leagues; fouth-weft from *St. Lucia*, thirty or thirty-five leagues; weft-fouth-weft from *Barbadoes*, fifty leagues; fouth-fouth-weft from *Martinico*, fifty leagues; fouth-fouth-weft from *Dominica*, fomewhat more than fixty leagues; weft-north-weft from *Tabago*, thirty-five, or according to fome charts, forty leagues; fouth from *St. Chriftopher*'s, one hundred leagues; and north from the *Spanifh* main, about thirty leagues.

It lies in the latitude of eleven degrees thirty minutes north, the fartheft to the fouth of any of the *Antilles*. We are not able to give its dimenfions with any degree of exactnefs, as not only authors but maps differ very much in regard thereto. We may however, without fear of erring much, affert that it is upwards of thirty *Englifh* miles in length, *De Lifle*'s map makes it near forty; and fifteen or fixteen in breadth, in fome places, though in others much lefs, and about twenty-five leagues in circumference. It appears from hence

hence to be twice as big as *Barbadoes*, larger than *St. Lucia, St. Vincent,* or *Tabago*; and, if we may take the words of some *French* memoir writers, contains of cultivatable land, near one third, of what is to be found in *Martinico*. These are circumstances of very great consequence, and though we cannot at present speak of them with precision, yet it cannot be long before we are properly and thoroughly instructed upon this subject, by those who have it in their power to treat it in the most authentic manner.

The situation of this island leaves us no room to doubt, that the climate is very warm, which, however, the *French* writers assure us, is very much moderated by the regular returns of the sea breeze, by which the air is rendered cool and pleasant. We may from the same authority assert, that it is wholsome; for though strangers especially are still liable to what is called the *Granada* fever, yet this is at present far from being so terrible as it formerly was; proves very rarely mortal, and as it chiefly proceeds from the humidity of the air, occasioned by the thickness of the woods, it will very probably be entirely removed, whenever the country is brought into a thorough state of cultivation, and this we may with the more boldness predict, as the same thing has constantly happened, in our own and in the *French* islands. Besides, the climate has some, and those too very peculiar advantages. The *seasons* as they are

are stiled in the *West-Indies*, are remarkably regular, the Blast is not hitherto known in this island; the inhabitants are not liable to many diseases, that are epidemic in *Martinico* and *Guadaloupe*; and, which is the happiest circumstance of all, it lies out of the track of the hurricanes, which with respect to the safety of the settlements on shore, and the security of navigation, is almost an inestimable benefit.

There are in *Granada* some very high mountains, but the number is small, and the eminencies scattered through it are in general rather hills, or as the *French* writers stile them *mornes*, gentle in their ascent, of no great height, fertile, and very capable of cultivation. But exclusive of these, there are on both sides the island, large tracts of level ground, very fit for improvement, the soil being almost every where, deep, rich, mellow, and fertile in the highest degree, so as to be equal in all respects, if not superior to that of any of the islands in the *West-Indies*, if the concurrent testimonies both of *French* and *British* planters may be relied upon. The former indeed have constantly in their applications to the *French* ministry insisted, that this might be very easily made one of the most valuable, though hitherto it has continued, for reasons which in part at least will hereafter appear, the weakest and the worst settled of all their colonies. This we find asserted at the very opening of the current century, in the memorials addressed to the council of state, confirmed

firmed some years afterwards by father *Labat*, and insisted upon with great vehemency, in representations which perhaps never reached the court, drawn up by very capable judges, the very last year that it continued to be a *French* island.

It is perfectly well watered by many streams of different sizes, and running in different directions, flowing, as some writers affirm, from a large lake on the summit of a high mountain, situated very near the center of the isle. There are also smaller brooks, running from most of the hills, and very fine springs almost every where, at a small distance from the shore. All these rivers abound with a great variety of excellent fish, and are resorted to by multitudes of water fowl. There are likewise in *Granada* several salt-ponds, which have also their uses and their value. But except that which has been before-mentioned, and another of which we shall hereafter speak, there are no lakes or standing waters of any considerable magnitude.

The great produce of this country, in its present condition, is a prodigious variety of all the different sorts of timber that are to be met with in any of the *West-India* islands, and all these excellent in their respective kinds; so that whenever this island comes to be tolerably cleared, vast profits will arise from the timber that may be cut down, and for which markets will not be wanting. There are likewise many rich fruits, valuable gums, dying woods, and several vegetable

getable products, such as oils, resins, balsoms, &c. which have always borne a very high price here, though we seldom had them so genuine, as we now may from hence. All the different kinds of ground provisions, which are so requisite to the subsistance of *West-India* plantations, are here in great quantities, and some kinds of grain ripen very kindly in this, which are either not raised at all, or are raised with difficulty in other islands. River and sea fish in great abundance, and in respect to the latter, turtle of the largest size and lamentins, which drew vessels from the other *French* islands for the sake of fishing. They have great plenty of all sorts of fowl, and prodigious quantities of game, ortolans, and a kind of red partridges especially. Besides these, the woods, are well furnished with many wild animals, that afford excellent food, and are very rarely met with in the other islands. They have likewise much cattle, and as their hills yield excellent pasture, if the country was better peopled, might have many more; so that we need not wonder, the *French* officers, who during the war, remained some time in this island, have represented it in so advantageous a light, and commended the great plenty in which they lived so highly, more especially in comparison of some other places.

But the distinguishing excellency of *Granada* does not lie simply in its great fertility, or in its fitness for a vast variety of valuable commodities;

but

but in the peculiar quality of its foil, which gives a furprizing and inconteftible perfection to all its feveral productions. The fugar of *Granada* is of a fine grain, and of courfe more valuable than that either of *Martinique* or *Guadaloupe*. The indigo, is the fineft in all the *Weft-Indies*. While tobacco remained the ftaple commodity, as once it was of thefe iflands, one pound of *Granada* tobacco was worth two or three that grew in any of the reft. The cacao and cotton have an equal degree of preheminence; nor is this founded fimply in the opinion of the *French*, but is equally known and allowed by the *Englifh* and *Dutch*; and in regard to the laft mentioned commodity, we may appeal to fome of the merchants of this city, who are well acquainted therewith, and upon whofe authority therefore we may the more fafely rely.

It is a point of juftice to obferve, that if credit be due to the memorials of *French* officers, who have vifited *Granada*, true *cinnamon* and fome *nutmeg-trees* are found there, which, if experience fhould verify, all that we have advanced in refpect to *Tabago*, may be as juftly applied to *Granada*; and the only reafon for infifting upon the fubject there, was becaufe we thought the fact better eftablifhed, from the authority of the *Dutch*, who of all nations are the beft acquainted with *fpices*. In refpect to fituation, and thofe expofitions that are effentially requifite to the proper culture of thefe valuable products, the iflands are every way equal,

or,

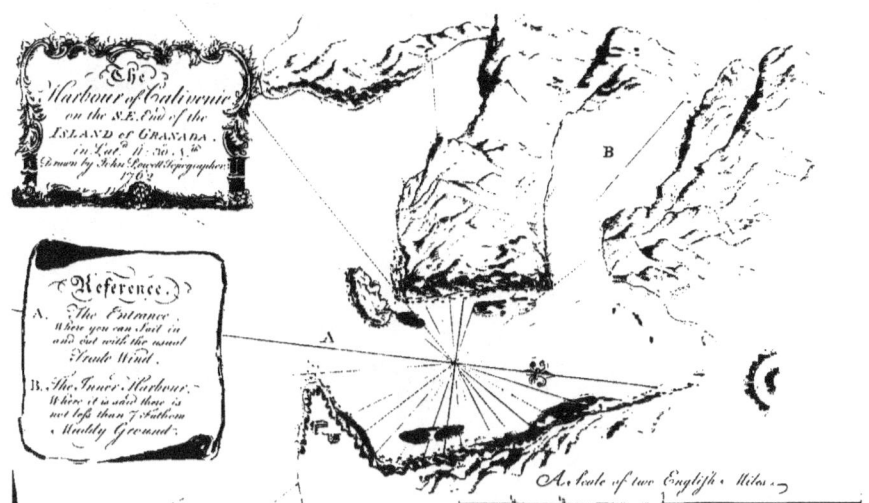

or, if upon making the experiment, *Granada* should be found preferable to *Tabago*, which, for a reason that will be hereafter assigned, may very probably prove the case, it ought no doubt to be preferred.

All the *French* writers agree, and those of our nation that have visited this island agree with them, that there is in general good anchoring ground, on all the coasts, and many commodious creeks and bays, both on the east and west side, which would be infinitely advantageous to commerce, if this country was fully peopled and compleatly cultivated; to which, they may be considered as a very powerful incitement, as islands might be mentioned, where the want of these conveniences, is no small drawback on the industry of the inhabitants. But besides these small, there are also two large ports of incomparable excellence, and which therefore deserve particular notice.

The first of these is the harbour of *Calivenie*, at the south-east extremity of the island, and is singularly safe and spacious. It consists of an outward, and an inward port. The former is three-quarters of a mile broad at its entrance, but widens as you advance, and becomes above a mile in extent within. As to the entrance of the interior port; it is about a quarter of a mile broad, but presently expands itself on both sides, so as to be very capacious, and has about seven fathom of water, with a soft muddy bottom, from whence seamen will easily judge of its utility. Ships lying here in the utmost safety, may from ware-houses on shore take in their lading very conveniently, and may then with great ease be hauled into the outer port, which has this peculiar advantage, that ships may either come into or go out of it with the ordinary trade wind. This port, supposing there was no other, in an island thus situated, and so very capable of being improved, would, to a trading nation like ours, render it a very valuable acquisition.

But the worth of *Granada* must be very highly enhanced, when we consider the other harbour which lies at the north-west end of the island, and is called the *Carenage*, the harbour of *Port Royal*, or the *Old Port*; which has been always esteemed one of the best harbours in the *West-Indies*, as possessing almost every advantage that can be desired. It is a full quarter of a mile broad at its entrance, and when once entered, it is so capacious, as to hold with ease a squadron of twenty-five ships of the line, where they may ride in perfect safety, in respect either to wind or weather. Besides, there lies, at a very small distance from this port, a lake of a considerable size, very deep, the water brackish, and which by cutting through a sand-bank might be very easily joined to the port, and would be then one of the finest basons in the world, and afford all the conveniences, that could possibly be wished, for careening the largest squadrons of the largest ships that we ever employ

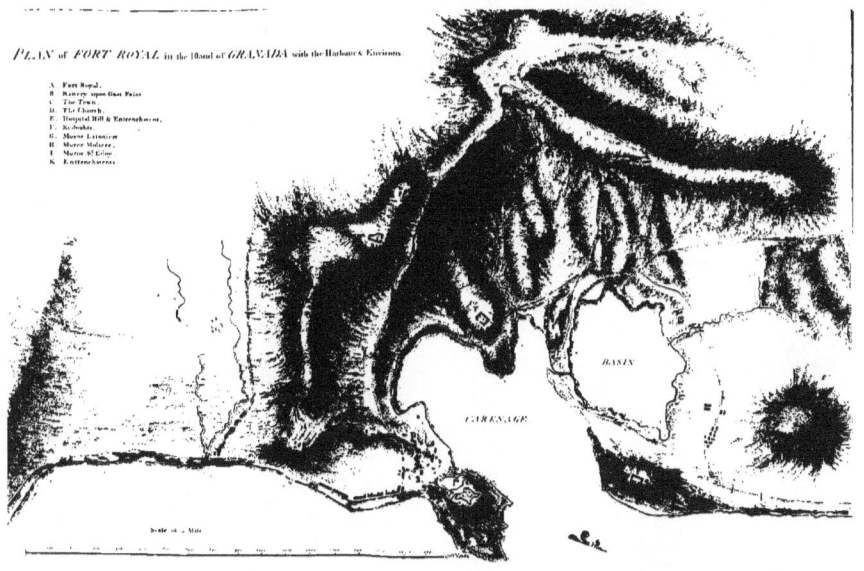

employ in this part of the world. The mouth of this port is secured by a tolerable fortress, called *Fort Royal*, where the governor resides, but the situation of it has been censured; and indeed there is no doubt, that by the help of two good fortifications, erected on the promontories which make the entrance of the harbour, it might be rendered inaccessible, since in case of an attack ships must warp in, under the fire of both fortresses, which would hardly be attempted. The benefits that may be justly expected from such a port as this, in an island so happily situated as this is, and producing such a variety of valuable commodities, are so obvious, that there is no need of entering into a detail of them. In time of war it would give us inexpressible advantages, against the *Spaniards* as well as the *French*; and, if it should ever happen, that by a multiplicity of services, our naval forces should be so divided, as to leave us only an inferior squadron in these parts, the *Carenage* would afford us a safe retreat, without obliging our ships to quit that station. A circumstance certainly very worthy of being regarded; and of which, the *French* availed themselves often, so long as this island remained in their possession.

This island was discovered by, and received its name from the famous Admiral *Christopher Columbus*, in his third voyage, in the year 1498. It was never occupied however by the *Spaniards*, chiefly for three reasons. *First*, Because the people in it were numerous and warlike; so that it might have proved no easy purchase. In the next place, they had continual wars with the *Indians* upon the continent; and it was an established maxim of the *Spanish* policy, never to hinder these nations from weakning one another. And *lastly*, Their possessions were so numerous, that they had no need of it.

The savages resorted in great numbers to this island, and were exceedingly attached thereto, as it furnished them plenty of subsistence in their way of hunting and fishing, was very happily situated, and afforded them the means of making several strong posts in the mountains; by which they were in hopes of maintaining it against any invaders. They lived in a constant correspondence with their countrymen in *Dominica* and *St. Vincents*, held in process of time a friendly correspondence with the *Spaniards*, and made frequent trips to the main, sometimes in a hostile manner, and at others, for the sake of acquiring certain fruits and dying woods, which they exchanged with the *Spaniards*. In this situation they were, when the *French* settled in *America*, who soon visited their island, and encouraged them to come to *Guadaloupe*.

This led the Baron *de Poincy*, who then commanded there, to think of establishing himself upon this isle so early as the year 1638. But the *Indians* however took their measures so well, that he was thoroughly convinced, it was an enterprize superior to his force, and therefore
very

very prudently declined it. In 1650 Mr. *du Parquet*, governor and proprietor of *Martinique*, formed the like defign, but previoufly made a purchafe of it, or at leaft of a right to eftablifh there, from the *Indians*. Accordingly he fent over a fmall colony, confifting of two hundred ftout men, who fortified themfelves as well as they could in the neighbourhood of the *Carenage*, and things went on for fome time amicably enough, between them and the natives. It was not long however before the latter repented of their bargain, and without notice or ceremony maffacred all the *French*, that were abroad felling timber or planting tobacco. There remained however a ftrength fufficient in the fettlement to revenge this infult; and they took their meafures with fo much precaution, that they furprized, and almoft utterly deftroyed the *Savages* on that fide the ifland. As for thofe who were on the other fide, they diffembled their fenfe of this carnage, the rather becaufe Mr. *du Parquet* fent a reinforement thither, of three hundred men. However, they only watched a favourable opportunity, which having found, they fuddenly entered through the paffes between the mountains, known only to themfelves, and fell upon the *French* with fuch fury, that they loft more in this than in the former infurrection. After this, they lived extremely upon their guard, till by repeated fupplies they thought themfelves in a condition to revenge this affront, and to rid themfelves effectually of these dangerous neighbours. This design they conducted with so much secrecy and prudence, that they surprized all their canoes, and those that were left to take care of them, before they endeavoured to storm the fastnesses of their enemies in the mountains; which they likewise performed with such success, that they drove them from all their posts, and gradually extirpated the whole race of *Indians* that were upon the island, not however without a considerable loss to themselves, and which was most to be regretted the death of the Sieur *le Comte*, cousin to Mr. *du Parquet*, whom he had appointed their governor, by whose sagacity this expedition had been planned, and who had shewn great spirit and resolution in carrying it into execution.

As soon as Mr. *du Parquet* was informed of this event, he sent over the Sieur *de Valmeniere* with the title of governor, and a small reinforcement. The officers in the colony headed by their major, whose name was *le Fort*, absolutely refused to receive him, and this, as they had a party amongst the inhabitants, produced a civil war; which, however, ended in favour of the governor, who reduced the male-contents, and made some of their chiefs prisoners. This insurrection once over, and the chiefs (the major excepted, who poisoned himself) banished, but without confiscation of their effects, or injury to their persons; the Sieur *de Valmeniere* applied himself with such vigour and vigilance, and at the same time with so much prudence and indulgence,

indulgence, to repairing the mischiefs which in the course of these troubles had befallen the colony, that in a very short space of time, the whole face of affairs was entirely changed. The old settlement was not only restored, but several new plantations were made, and exclusive of great quantities of tobacco, they began to raise both very fine indigo and excellent cotton.

In consequence of the encouragements he gave, and his mild and moderate manner of proceeding, his colony not only flourished, but the number of its inhabitants increased; many resorting thither, who had been less fortunate in their other islands, bringing with them slaves, and for those times, a perfect knowledge of the art of planting, they quickly repaired all their past losses, and grew imperceptibly into easy circumstances. The report of this was extremely welcome to the proprietor Mr. *du Parquet*, whose fortune by his many purchases, and bearing the charge of several expensive expeditions, was both impaired and embarrassed. He took care therefore, to have a very clear representation drawn up, of the several commodities here produced, the number of new settlers, and other circumstances of advantage, by which it appeared the most thriving and the most promising of all their *West-India* isles. This account therefore being transmitted to *Paris*, produced that favourable effect which he desired, insomuch that large offers were made for his property; and at length closing with the proposals made

made by the Count *de Cerillac* and his son, *Granada* and all its dependancies were sold to them in 1657, for ninety thousand livres.

These gentlemen might certainly have been very great gainers by this purchase, if they had, which had been the surest way, either continued the old governor, or instructed the person they sent over, strictly to follow his plan. But their new governor was the very reverse of the Sieur *de Valmeniere*, and either through the haughtiness and severity of his own temper, or in compliance with the instructions received from the new proprietors; he acted in so arbitrary a manner, that all the people of substance speedily quitted the island, and the rabble who were left behind by their not having it in their power to quit it, took a short resolution, to be quit of him. A general revolt ensued. The governor was seized and imprisoned, brought to a trial before judges who were none of them able to write, and condemned to suffer death. He insisted, as a gentleman, upon being beheaded; but as no-body could be found to perform the execution in that manner, they directed him to be shot. As soon as the news of this arrived in *France*, a ship of force was sent with a commissary on board, who had express orders to make an exact inquiry into the whole affair, and do strict justice upon the offenders. On his arrival however the commissary found this absolutely impracticable, there were but a few people left, and they were all alike guilty;

in

in confequence of which, they all efcaped punifhment. This impunity, though neceffary, was very far from having a good effect; the defertion continued, and the ifland would have been totally abandoned, if the Count *de Cerillac* and his fon had not been obliged to part with their property, to the company erected in 1664. The directors of this fociety faved *Granada*, for they very fpeedily fent proper people thither, refettled the old plantations, and very probably would have carried things much farther than they had hitherto been ever carried, if they had not been fuppreffed by *Lewis* XIV. in 1674. This gave a new check to the colony, and revived the former difturbances, which though they were very foon quelled, yet were followed from an ill impreffion of the new adminiftration, by the defertion of fome of the more opulent planters.

Thus in the fhort fpace of *twenty-four* years, the inhabitants of *Granada*, were expofed to two maffacres by the *Indians*, three infurrections of the planters themfelves, and five changes in their government. The ifland henceforward belonged to the King, who fent a governor thither, and after the public tranquility was reftored, the people began again to thrive, but more flowly, from the memory of paft misfortunes, and their not being totally free from apprehenfions of the like happening again. They went on however with their plantations, and, which muft appear very fingular, they fuffered

fome

some *Indian* families, to settle again amongst them. These were chiefly from *Dominica*, and their principal motive for receiving them was, the entertaining by their assistance some kind of commerce with the natives upon the main; by which they obtained occasionally, considerable quantities of cochineal, balsam of *Tolu*, and *Capachu* oil, commodities which they found means to vend with no small advantage. At the same time we must observe, that with a greater degree of industry and attention, they might have had all these, and many other articles of still superiour value at home. But with all this, and though their affairs certainly grew better, yet they were very far from answering the expectations that had been formed, which arose from a variety of causes. They were not constantly supplied from, and never had a regular correspondence with their mother country. The practices of the *farmers-general* ruined their staple commodity of *tobacco*, and the *African* company sold them slaves at a very high rate. These inconveniences obliged them to have recourse to an expedient, very much facilitated by their situation, which was entering into a close correspondence with their neighbours the *Dutch*, who first put them upon raising sugar, furnished them with the means, and took that and the rest of the commodities of the country in payment, which of course lessened their returns to *France*. Yet all this time, the *French* court were very far from being unapprized of the importance

portance of this ifland, and the improvements that might be made in it; of which many of their commercial writers boafted, while their political fyftem at home hindered them from ever taking any effectual fteps towards the promoting the interefts of a colony, that would have amply repaid any cofts that might have been beftowed upon it. Thefe are circumftances, which though not either ufelefs or unentertaining, are acknowledged to be lefs important in the light of hiftorical facts, than in that of political cautions.

The ingenious father *Labat* was here in 1705, and, though he did not remain long, yet he made fome curious and pertinent remarks. He fpeaks of the planters as eafy in their circumftances, though not very polifhed in their manners. He clearly difcerned, that great improvements might be made in fo pleafant and fertile a country, and regretted that the *French* refugees from their ruined colony of *St. Chriftophers* were not fent hither, where they would quickly have repaired their own loffes, and have rendered this colony at the fame time much more ufeful to *France*. He made fome other reflections, which the reader will read with equal pleafure and furprize. " If, fays he, *Barbadoes* had a
" port, as fafe, as capacious, as commodious,
" and as eafy to be fortified, it would be in-
" deed an incomparable ifland; the *Englifh*
" know much better than we, how to turn
" every natural advantage in their iflands to
" the

"the utmoſt; and, if *Granada* had belonged "to them, it had before now changed its ap- "pearance, it had been long ago a rich "and powerful colony, inſtead of which, we "have hitherto reaped little, from thoſe bene- "ficial circumſtances from which vaſt profits "might have ariſen, ſince after ſo many years "poſſeſſion, the country is yet in a manner de- "ſert, thinly peopled, without commodities, "having little commerce, their habitations or "rather cabins mean, ill built, worſe furniſh- "ed; and, to ſay all in a word, in a very little "better ſtate, than when Mr. *du Parquet* "bought it from the *Savages*."

We muſt however admit, that within the half century that has ſince paſt, ſomewhat more attention has been paid to this iſland, and its productions have turned within this period much more to the account of *France*. They had ſent for ſome years before it came into our hands thither, twelve thouſand hogſheads of ſugar annually, beſides coffee, cacao, and a large quantity of excellent cotton. Yet it is generally allowed, that never one half of the country was properly ſettled, nor half the profits drawn from what was ſettled, that might have been obtained, if the inhabitants had been better planters, and had been alſo better ſupplied with ſlaves. The repreſentations made to the *French* court treat all the improvements made there as very imperfect, as demonſtrative rather of the fertility of the ſoil, and the excellence

lence of the climate, than of the industry of the inhabitants. These papers likewise suggest, that many other improvements might have been introduced, and that some lucrative branches of commerce might have been easily opened from thence. It has been said the late Marshal *Saxe* had a grant of this island; which, if true, might have been given him as an equivalent for *Tabago*, as he looked upon himself to have a kind of title to the Duchy of *Courland*. According to the accounts of our own people, who have resided there, and the Captains of men of war who have visited it; the *French* have not been extravagant in their accounts, or visionary in their speculations. An *English* gentleman who has had great opportunities of knowing, thinks as much sugar is raised here as in *Barbadoes*; which is not at all impossible, though it did not find a regular passage to *France*. In a short time, all these difficulties will be cleared up, and we shall know its produce with much greater certainty, than perhaps it was ever known to its former masters.

But, exclusive of these productions, it was of great utility to the *French*, during the course of the last war, when the single ships of force they sent to the *West-Indies*, with the transports under their care, came regularly hither, with little danger of falling into the hands of our cruisers. Here they remained in safety, and from hence they sent supplies of men, ammunition, and provisions, in small vessels, which

creeping

creeping along the *Grenadillas*, *St. Vincent*, and *St. Lucia*, arrived, generally speaking, safely in the harbour of *St. Peter*'s in *Martinique*. In this respect, as well as in many others, the *French* will very sensibly feel the loss of this island, as we shall the advantage arising from the possession of it. A *British* squadron stationed here will be, as has been already hinted, a severe and continual check upon the *Spaniards* as well as the *French*; so that undoubtedly, when they gave this isle and all its dependencies for *St. Lucia*, they had no very clear conceptions of the consequences that might result from such an exchange, either to themselves or their allies; consequences however, that we may truly affirm are obvious and indisputable, which therefore cannot fail of being justified in the event. It would be very easy to expatiate upon this subject, in a manner that might be very pleasing to a *British* reader, as it would incontestably prove that the *French* are not always too hard for us in negotiation. But at this juncture, such a discussion would for many reasons be very imprudent, and shall be therefore omitted. The present point is to know the value of what we have got, and by what means these new possessions are to be best kept and improved; for, if we attend steadily and properly to these, their importance will certainly appear in a much stronger light, than either ourselves or our neighbours conceive possible. Things will then speak, and speak loudly for themselves, and
till

till then it is best to be modest and silent about them.

There runs from the southern extremity of the isle of *Granada*, in the direction of north by east, a long range of little *islets*, extending about twenty leagues. These are of different sizes, but all of them, except the *Round* island, very small. They have narrow channels between them, only passable by boats, and very dangerous even in these, to those who are not perfectly acquainted with their nature. We are informed by *John de Laet*, that the natives call this string of islands *Begos*; the *Spaniards* imposed upon them the name of *Grenadillas*; the *French* stile them *Grenadilles* or *Grenadines*; our countrymen in the *West-Indies* usually call them the *Grenades*; and as their coasts are rocky, and the access dangerous, they generally keep to the windward of them, in order to avoid accidents; which however when the weather is thick and hazy, but too frequently happens.

The number of these islands is very incertain, but according to the best information, there may be about three-and-twenty of them, capable of cultivation. The soil being remarkably rich, the climate pleasant, and all the necessaries of life, whenever they shall be settled, will be easily obtained. According to the sentiments of the best judges, large quantities of indigo, coffee, and cotton, may be raised upon them, nor are they at all unfit for sugar. It is however thought improper to attempt the

planting

planting of canes, from an apprehension that in time of war they might be liable to the insults of privateers, as their size would hardly admit of a sufficient number of inhabitants to defend them. In their present situation, they abound in excellent timber, of which the *French* made little use, as they met with an easier and better supply from *St. Lucia*. In former times, they were very serviceable to our planters in *Barbadoes*, who cut great quantities of mill-timber, which was a very great conveniency. But for many years past the *French* have not only prevented this, as injurious to their property, but by stationing guard-ships upon the coast, made prize, in time of full peace, of all *English* vessels they found at anchor there, and even of such as appeared in sight of them; which was a very great detriment to our navigation. For, if vessels bound to *Barbadoes*, either through thick weather or being disabled, missed that island, and ran down the south side of it, which was the common route, they came of course upon these islands, and fell into the hands of these guard-ships; the apprehension of which, made them so cautious, as to render their voyages to that island longer and more tedious than in former times. But as all these difficulties will be removed for the future, and as the clearing of these isles in order to their cultivation, will be an immediate and considerable advantage to the inhabitants of *Barbadoes*, these

circumstances

circumstances evidently enhance the value of this acquisition.

There are besides these, *five* larger islands, which not only in point of size, but in many other respects are more considerable, and therefore deserve particular notice. The first of these, that is, the nearest to the line of islets before-mentioned, retains the *Indian* name of *Cariouacou*, it is of a circular figure, about six or seven leagues in compass, lies five leagues east from *Granada*; fourteen south-west from *St. Vincent*; and about forty leagues west-south-west from *Barbadoes*. This little isle, is represented by the *French* who have visited it, as one of the finest and most fruitful spots in *America*; the soil remarkably fertile, and from its being pervaded by the sea breeze, the climate equally wholsome and pleasant. It is covered with valuable timber, interspered with rich fruit-trees, and when settled and cultivated, is capable of all kinds of improvement. But the circumstance by which it is most distinguished, is its having as deep, capacious, and commodious an harbour, as any in the *West-Indies*, and on this account, has more than once been recommended to the *French* government, as a place capable of being made of much superior utility, to islands of far greater extent, and even allowing these to have equal merit, in regard to the value and the variety of their productions.

About a league north-east from *Cariouacou*, lies what the *French* call, *l'Isle de l'Union*, tho' in truth there are two, the larger three leagues, and the lesser, two in length. At the distance of two leagues from these, lies *Cannouan* or *Caouanne,* so called from the great resort thither of the kind of tortoises or sea-turtle, to which the *Indians,* and after them the *French,* give this name. This island is three leagues in length, and one and a half broad, and has a small islet to the west of it. At the distance of two leagues from this, lies the *Isle de Moustiques,* or *Moskito Island*; three leagues in breadth, and one in length. All these islands, are allowed to be pleasant, wholsome, and exceedingly fruitful. They are at present over-grown with different kinds of timber; some of which are become exceedingly scarce in the other isles, and some also, which bear, at present a very high price in *Europe.*

At the distance of a league from *Moskito Island,* lies *Becovya, Bequia,* or *Bekia,* which is but two leagues south-west from *St. Vincent.* This is the largest of all the isles dependant upon *Granada,* being about twelve leagues in circumference, and consequently somewhat larger than *Montserrat.* The soil is equal if not superior to any of the rest, it has likewise a very safe and convenient port. But with all these advantages, it has some very signal defects. It has no considerable eminencies, little, (at least it is so said) if any fresh water, and is full of venomous reptiles; for which reason the *French* call it *Little Martinique*; and therefore very rarely

rarely frequent it, except fishing upon its coasts, which brought them to be so well acquainted with its harbour, represented by them as land-locked on every side, easy in its entrance, and very deep and capacious, and in which their small armaments frequently took shelter, during the last war, in proceeding as we have before-mentioned, from *Granada* to *Port St. Peter*'s in the island of *Martinico*, and this circumstance hereafter may possibly merit for it more attention.

But though, except in the cases before-mentioned, so little regarded by the *French*, it is however freqently visited by the *Savages* from *Dominica* and *St. Vincents*, for the sake of the little gardens, they have there, which are very neatly kept, and in which they have a great variety of very fine fruits; particulary the *ananas* or *pine-apple*, remarkably large and very high flavoured. The *Grenadillas*, as the *Spaniards* name it; the *Rhang-apple*, as it is stiled by the *Dutch*; or as we call it the *passion-flower*, which produces also an excellent fruit, full of a fine red juice, extremely cooling and refreshing in fevers, and *water-melons* of the largest size, the most delicate in taste of any in the *West-Indies*. In this isle also, there are a great variety of those climbing plants or creepers, which the *French* call *liannes*; and among these, there are two that have very remarkable properties. The one is stiled *lianne a sang*, or the *bloody creeper*, because when it is cut, there issues from it a crimson liquor,

liquor, that tinges linnen of a bright scarlet. The other, they call *lianne jaune*, because the juice of that dyes in the like manner a deep yellow. There is likewise in this isle a very singular kind of snail, called *Burgans de teinture*; they are of the bigness of the top of the finger, resembling in most repects a common snail, which have an upper and an under shell; the former of a dusky blue, and the latter of a bright silver colour, spotted here and there with abundance of black specks. The flesh of this snail is very white, but the intestines (probably from the fruit on which it feeds) are of so deep a red, as to be seen through its body. When a few of these snails are put into a deep plate, and shaken together, they eject a quantity of slimy matter of a purple colour; in which, if linnen be dipped, it takes first a violet, then a scarlet, and when dry becomes of a bright purple. This like the colours from the liannes before-mentioned, are apt to run in washing, and to wear out by degrees. Yet the *French* assert, that by dissolving a small quantity of alum in lemon juice, steeping linnen or calicoe in it, and then drying it carefully in the shade, before it is dipped in any of these juices, and when thoroughly impregnated with them, again carefully dried, the colours remain well fixed, and lose little or nothing of their beauty. They have also in this isle the *tunal*, which seems to be a species of the opuntia or nopal, which in our isles is commonly stiled (though the fruit is really a kind of fig) the

the *prickle-pear*, and when the fruit is full ripe, is covered with a multitude of little worms, which being carefully gathered and dried, yeild a colour of the same kind, and very little if at all inferior to the *cochineal*.

These are mentioned only as slight, indeed very slight specimens of the valuable things, which this island, so considerable in point of size, though hitherto disregarded, may in process of time afford. They are not however so much mentioned as matter of information, as in the light of hints for enquiry. This disposition of exploring accurately the commercial articles which human skill derives from the several productions of nature, is of singular utility, whereever it is prudently and steadily employed, but in new acquisitions more especially, because in them new objects continually occur. It frequently leads to fresh materials for industry, fresh improvements in arts, and fresh subjects for commerce. Discoveries no less important in their nature and consequences, than the discovery of new countries, since these are only valuable as they contribute to those ends. Such enquiries by giving a right turn to curiosity, render that quality of the mind, which improperly exerted is always useless, often injurious, highly serviceable and wonderfully beneficial. By this means, the talents of all who go to the plantations, with whatever view and in whatever capacity, become equally useful to the plantations. For the observations of a super-cargo,

cargo, of an engineer, of a land as well as of a sea officer, of an intelligent sailor, a sensible mechanic, or an attentive domestic, in the space of a very short residence, may contribute as much or perhaps more, to the prosperity of a settlement, and by that means to the welfare of the mother country, than if he had spent his whole life-time there, in the hardest labour. A circumstance, that if it was not so very obvious and incontestable in the eye of reason, might be very easily and beyond all contradiction proved, from the evidence of facts and the lights of experience.

After so copious a description of these islands, and particularly of the last, it is presumed that the removing hither, if that should be found either necessary or expedient, the nation of free *Indians* from *St. Vincents*, will appear a thing very practicable. It is no conclusive argument even against *Bequia*, that it has been reputed uninhabitable for want of water, because the same thing was long said with regard to *Antego*, which is nevertheless a well inhabited and well cultivated island at this day. When this country comes to be more strictly examined than hitherto it has ever been, it will very probably be found, that though deficient in rivulets, it may not be absolutely without water; but that springs and wells, may supply the uses of *Indians*, though they might not be sufficient for the service of a colony, which must be supported, by the industry of its inhabitants in their plantations.

tations. It would not probably be very difficult to perfuade the *Indians* to leave *St. Vincent*, for an ifland at leaft equal in extent to all that they can poffefs there, with which they are perfectly well acquainted, and where they might live in fafety, after their own manner and undifturbed by ftrangers. It may appear from, and it was the principal intention of producing, thofe fpecimens, that without departing much from their ufual employments, thefe people might be there of great ufe to themfelves and to their *Britifh* neighbours. We know that they have raifed provifions plentifully for the *French*; and they might collect things very valuable to us with as little labour, and procure as great or greater benefits in exchange for themfelves, than ever they did from that nation. This would occafion a refort to the port, and a conftant intercourfe with them, which would be attended with many obvious advantages, and in procefs of time, may very probably produce many more than can be forefeen at prefent. Juftice, humanity, and good ufage, would certainly work upon the minds of thefe people, and there is no doubt to be made, that the profits which might be drawn from the fpontaneous fervices of a free people, would be an acquifition equal in point of value, to the tract of country whatever it may be, that for this purpofe we fhould be induced to fpare them. It is a truth, and a truth of fuch importance, that it can never be too often or too seriously inculcated, that the attaching these people to us, in preference to all the other *European* nations, who possess dominions in the *West-Indies*, would be attended with the most salutary as well as the most beneficial consequences. Naked, barbarous, despicable, as they are, they are still human creatures, and that in the faculties of their minds, as well as in the form of their bodies; so that if we could happily fall upon a method of binding them to our interests, by making them sensible of their own, we should gradually lead them to the support, from their participating in the advantages, of society. The *French* have on the continent, had a very visible superiority over us in this respect, by means of their *missionaries*; but they do not so much as pretend to have succeeded in any degree, in the conversion of these people, with respect to whom probably we may more easily prevail, by cherishing their love of liberty; and at the same time conducting them gently and almost insensibly, to the true principles of humanity, which when taught rather by example than precept, and managed with discretion and indulgence, they will by degrees become men, which is naturally, indeed necessarily, the first step to their becoming *christians*.

It was the consideration of these islands dependant upon that of *Grenada*, which led to the question whether they might not be, all circumstances considered, more proper for the introduction of spices, than even the island of *Tabago*? The five islands of the *Meluccas*, which

which are *Ternate, Tydor, Motier, Maquien,* and *Bacham,* were so many separate kingdoms, rich and full of inhabitants, before they were known to the *Europeans,* lie all in a line like these, and are none of them larger than *Carioua-cou.* They have small straits of the sea between them like the *Grenades,* bear the same trees, herbs, and roots, are some of them dificient in fresh water, and produced originally, *cinnamon* and *nutmegs* as well as *cloves,* the uses as well as the method of cultivating and curing of which were taught them by the *Chinese,* as Dr. *Argensola,* who wrote an excellent history of the *Molucca* islands, informs us. *Banda,* where the nutmegs originally grew, is not above half the size of *Bequia*; and *Amboyna,* to which the *Dutch* seem at present inclined to confine both *nutmegs* and *cloves,* is rather inferior in point of extent to the island of *Grenada.* It is indeed true, that *Tabago* lies more remote; and of consequence the spice trade, if it could be settled there, might be better preserved and more effectually confined. But however, these points of fact, while the matter still remains in speculation only, deserve to be thoroughly known, that they may be maturely weighed, before we actually attempt to carry a scheme of this sort into execution; the success of which will, in a great measure depend, on precautions taken at the beginning.

The reader will decide for himself, as to the nature and justice of the equivalent given us in *Grenada* and its dependant islands, for that of *St. Lucia,*

*Lucia*, when in his own mind he shall have run a parallel between the two islands, which with that intention have been exactly and impartially described. In doing this, he will compare their respective extents, and the capacity of each of them for improvement; he will advert to their respective situations, and call to mind the consequences that naturally flow from them; he will maturely weigh the strength of each island, and the means that from thence arise of defending it; he will consider their ports, the condition in which they are at present, and the facility with which they may be put into a better; he will reflect upon their importance, in all the different lights of war, of peace, and of commerce; he will remember that *Grenada* and its dependances, are free from *hurricanes*; to which by the way our island of *St. Vincent* also is very seldom exposed; and he will distinguish between the degrees of evidence, relative to the several advantages and defects of both, as they arise from certainty or supposition, from probabilities and facts, from what may be reasonably conjectured, and from what is put beyond all conjecture, by the lights of experience. But above all, he will be pleased to bear in mind, that the *honour* of the crown of *Great Britain*, in respect to her title to *St. Lucia* is fully secured, from the very nature of this exchange; that her *interests* in respect to her obtaining a sugar island, a proper extent of territory, and in that, the benefit of commodious ports, has been likewise wife attended to; and he will also take this material circumstance into his thoughts, that if it had been even best, to have kept *St. Lucia*, the possession not only of that, but of all the other neutral, now become *British* islands, would have been very much endangered, if the *French* had retained the possession of *Grenada*, with all those islets and isles that are dependant upon it; and by that means had been put under an inevitable and pressing necessity of considering and making the most of the numerous advantages which they afford. These hints of inquiry being pursued as well as premised, there can be no doubt, that he will form a proper decision upon this truly important point.

We are now to close this detail of facts, and the various observations that have been raised upon them, with a few general remarks, relative to the whole; and which are principally calculated, to explain the true value, and to ascertain the real importance of those islands, that are now become ours. This can be only done, by contemplating them in different lights, that is, in those several and separate points of view, from which they may every one of them become more or less, immediately or remotely, directly or indirectly, assisting to the interests, increasing the power, augmenting the commerce, extending the navigation, and thereby promoting the welfare of *Great Britain*; or, in other words, conducing to the industry, the independency, and the happiness, of their fellow-low citizens and fellow subjects, who are the inhabitants of this their MOTHER COUNTRY.

These are the great ends, these the ultimate design of COLONIES, these are the benefits, these are the emoluments, that are to be expected from them, in return for all that charge and trouble, that is necessary in settling them; that pains and attention, which is ever requisite to raise, maintain, and support them; and that immense expence of blood as well as treasure, which is sometimes necessary, to protect and defend them. In the last age, as we have fully seen, wise men foresaw the prodigious assistance, the innumerable advantages, that might be derived to this nation, from distant settlements. Events that cannot lie, and have therefore a just title to be believed, have clearly, and in the most convincing manner demonstrated, that in thinking thus they thought right. What was speculation then, is experience now. The single question therefore that remains to be discussed in relation to the *West-Indies*, is how far our new acquisitions will answer all these desirable purposes, and therefore this is the last that we shall attempt to discuss.

In the first place let us consider, that general arrangement of things, which has taken place in this part of the world. There is not now an island small or great, indeed scarce a rock in the *West-Indies*, the right to as well as the possession of which, is not clearly ascertained, and this without introducing any new powers into that part of the world, which must have been
exceedingly

exceedingly prejudicial to our interests. By thus adjusting the settlements of different powers, an end is put, at least as far as human foresight reaches, to all their ambitious views, to the self-interested projects of private persons, and to the schemes of enterprizing governors, which have been the principal sources of those disputes, that have at different seasons been so destructive to every different nation in its turn.

In virtue of this authentic and absolute settlement, many of our old plantations will avail themselves of those supplies of timber, from which they have been for many years precluded. The run-away *Negroes* will not be able to shelter themselves any more in uninhabited islands, and those impediments to and embarrassments of our navigation, which have been so severely felt, and in consequence of which so many loud complaints have been made to almost every government in our colonies, will be now effectually removed, by the taking away of the causes, without which they must probably have continued for ever.

By this means, illicit commerce will be lessened at least, if not entirely prevented. It will be a great encouragement to industry, by the taking away those temptations to persons of unsettled tempers of roving into islands under no settled government, where of course men were at liberty to pursue their private advantage, at the expence of the public interest. From the same reasons, we may expect that *piracy*, which has

has so often and so terribly afflicted the honest planters and the fair traders in the *West-Indies*, will never more revive, as all the ports and places to which these lawless people were wont to resort, will no longer exist, at least in the manner they did; and this as it will be an advantage in common to the colonies of every nation, so to ours in particular, who suffered most by these sort of depredations, from the value and extent of our commerce, which rendered us more frequently a prey to these enemies of mankind.

We shall have, in virtue of this regulation, a new and a very considerable province in the *West-Indies*, composed of islands exceedingly well situated in all respects, as well for their correspondence with each other, as for their general intercourse with *Great Britain*. These in their infancy, will be sheltered by the force that there is at present in *Barbadoes*, and in proportion as they become better settled, they will in their turns be enabled to send assistance to that island, or as that is the usual rendezvous of our expeditions, will be in a condition to furnish their respective quotas, when necessary in succeeding times. To this we may add, that our old settlements, may now disburthen their supernumerary inhabitants on territories belonging to their mother country, instead of going as it is notorious that great numbers have done, to *Danish* and *Dutch* settlements; by which means also, some quantities of land in the isles we have always

always possessed, may be converted to the feeding of cattle and raising provisions, for which they are much wanted, and are also much fitter than being under canes, where by producing incertain crops, they serve only to discourage industry, by impoverishing their owners.

By this new distribution of property, we are brought much nearer to the *Spanish* main; and this in time of peace, may enable us to furnish them with supplies of *Negroes* and other necessaries, which hitherto they have received from the *French* and *Dutch*, perhaps upon higher terms. In time of war again, we have from these islands, such evident and such effectual means of keeping their fleets in awe, interrupting all correspondence between their settlements, and making descents upon their coasts, as with the experience of their past losses, will very probably discourage that wary nation from breaking hastily again, with those who have them so much more in their power, and may very easily embarrass and interrupt their commerce, with very little hazard, and, comparatively speaking, with no expence to themselves.

In the next place, let us advert to the alterations this new distribution has made, in regard to the *French* power in these parts. It has been plainly made appear in the progress of this discourse, that they will lose the conveniency of raising vast quantities of fresh provisions, as well as considerable supplies of valuable commodities, which they continually and constantly

received

received from those that were then stiled neutral, but so far as this went, were really *French* islands. They will in like manner lose the advantages of felling timber, and building sloops and even larger vessels in *Dominica* and *St. Vincent*, as they were accustomed to do. Besides, they will be deprived of their communication with the *Indians* in the one, and with the *Indians* and free *Negroes* in the other of these islands, from whence they derived, as our countrymen in those parts well know, and they themselves confess, such services as were productive of various advantages, exclusive of the check they kept upon us. They will no longer enjoy the turtle and lamentin fishing round the coasts of *Tabago*, which was their annual resort, but will for the future be confined within the bounds, and to the coasts of their own islands.

These circumstances, when taken together, will bring very sensible difficulties upon their planters, by constraining them to employ greater pains, and a larger number of hands, for procuring those necessary supplies, which they formerly received in great abundance, with little trouble and very small expence. It will likewise follow, as all who are acquainted with these countries must know, that from being thus streightned, they will be compelled to the employing more *Negroes*; and yet even with this increase of slaves, less work will be done in their sugar plantations than formerly, when almost all their wants with respect to subsistance, and

and even with regard to buildings, were supplied upon such easy terms. In this situation also as many vessels of different sizes were continually occupied in their intercourse with these isles, with which they can now have no farther connection, their navigation must be diminished, and will of course decline. A circumstance that hereafter and in the progress of events, will be found of much greater consequence than either they apprehend, or ourselves can conceive at present. For in this as in many other respects, TIME, the best commentator upon transactions of this nature, will make numerous discoveries, that lie now beyond the discernment even of the most penetrating politicians.

By parting with *Granada* and its dependancies, they have not only lost the produce in sugar, coffee, cotton, &c. of that island, which was very considerable; with all title to those improvements, which as has been shewn from their own authors, they were fully convinced might be made therein; and the advantage of those safe and commodious ports, which have been already described, but likewise the facility which they derived from thence, of succouring all their other islands, even when we had superior squadrons in those seas; to which for the future, they must in case of a war be inevitably exposed. By the same step, they have deprived themselves on that side at least, of the intercourse they had with the *Spaniards*, and must hereafter run much greater hazards than formerly, in receiving, when their necessities require them, supplies of provisions and military stores from the *Dutch*. These are points, upon which we barely touch; but which if it was proper, we might expatiate on, in terms that would sufficiently discover, that in this respect they made a much greater sacrifice, than was perhaps evident to their ministers in *Europe*.

The proportion between the property, and consequently between the power of the two nations, in the *West-Indies*, is now extremely altered. For not to repeat what has been already said, of their being despoiled of those plantations they had surreptitiously made, on the islands of *Dominica* and *St. Vincent*; which might however with great justice be taken into the account, we will confine ourselves to the islands in the actual possession of both crowns, before and since the conclusion of the peace. Our property in the former period, compared to theirs, was no more than as *one* to *five*; whereas it is now almost as *ten* to *fifteen*, or nearly as *two* to *three*. If therefore, when we were in so much a weaker state, we were still able to protect even the smallest of our islands, during all the late wars between the two crowns, from being so much as insulted, and in a condition in the very last, to conquer almost all theirs; shall we have any reason to fear what may hereafter happen, when in consequence of settling our new acquisitions, we shall have acquired, as we necessarily must, so large an accession of force?

But

But this is not all. The situation and disposition of our islands give us, in respect to this power, still farther and greater advantages. Our northern islands will remain what they always have been, a perpetual check to them on that side. *Dominica* lies, as we have shewn, in the very center of their possessions, so as to command and to distress the navigation equally of *Martinico* and *Guadaloupe*. At the southern extremity again, we have *Granada* and all the islands belonging to it, connected with *St. Vincent*, from whence we have an easy and constant correspondence with *Barbadoes*, and a number of safe and commodious ports, to which our fleets may at all times resort; and these circumstances taken together may certainly banish the apprehensions of any danger to our old or new colonies, in case of a future rupture with *France*.

We ought next to shew, what those benefits are, that will probably result from these new acquisitions, to the present and to future ages. It will however be previously necessary to observe, that upon the first view some prejudices may arise, from the smallness of these islands, which are in truth very diminutive, if put into the balance with the *French*, and still more so, if they should be compared with those that the *Spaniards* possess in the *West-Indies*. It does not however follow from thence, that they are either insignificant or inconsiderable. It may be, when we come to examine this matter more attentively, we shall find, that this very circumstance,

P 2           which

which strikes superficial observers in one light, will appear to competent and candid judges, in quite another; so that instead of furnishing matter for a solid objection, it may, when maturely weighed, be found the strongest recommendation; if it can be proved, that in regard to colonies in this part of the world especially, small islands have the greatest advantages.

In the first place then, they enjoy a purer air, from the sea breeze passing constantly over them, and when cleared of superfluous wood, as they must be in order to their cultivation, continually pervading them. This we see is a natural effect, arising from the very circumstance of their size, and must of necessity render the climate at once more temperate and more wholsome. The soil too, in these small islands, is more fertile, more capable of being manured, and in many respects more easily cultivated, than in larger islands, and which is a point very essential to the matter under our consideration; they are from this circumstance also, capable of being more easily, more speedily, and more compleatly settled, than if their extent was larger: all of which are real and incontestible advantages.

Besides, from the vicinity of the sea on every side, and the facility of fishing round their coasts, the inhabitants of such islands derive the means of constantly supplying themselves, with a very considerable part of their subsistance, with very little labour and at an easy expence,

with

with this additional benefit, that the advantages arising from thence, which could not be the case in a large country, are alike common to all the inhabitants. This extent of coast in proportion to that of territory, as we have already more than once remarked, is also very favourable to commerce, as might be shewn in a great variety of instances, if it was not too obvious to stand in need of any explanation. It is no less apparent, that such islands for the very same reason, that makes them easier settled, are also easier defended, which is another point of very high consequence to the colony and to the mother country.

The islands of which we are speaking, have over and above these general advantages, some that are peculiar to themselves, and which are likewise of no small importance. They are, as appears from the description of each of them, exceedingly well watered, and this by running streams, which will afford their inhabitants the conveniency of erecting water-mills, machines that are more useful and less expensive, than either wind-mills, or those in which cattle are employed. The ridges of hills from which these rivulets run, render the *seasons* more regular in these islands, and, there is at least a strong probability, will exempt them, if not totally, yet in a very great degree, from short crops, the heaviest of all misfortunes to a planter, and to which the *French* as well as our own islands are very frequently subject.

As these natural privileges of small islands are thus capable of being demonstrated by reason, so the effects that might be expected from them, are justified likewise from experience. If we consider the larger islands in the hands of the *French*, we shall find that their produce, however considerable, is not in proportion to the extent of country, as the *French* writers themselves very candidly acknowledge, and as our countrymen who have been upon those islands, and have carefully attended to this particular, likewise admit. The same thing is yet more visible, in regard to the *Spaniards*, who possess at once islands the largest and the least profitable in the *West-Indies*. The *Dutch*, on the other hand, have found means to render the smallest, and in point of soil and climate, the worst islands in the *West Indies*, by dint of skill and of industry wonderfully flourishing, exceedingly populous, and of course highly beneficial.

Yet in this respect, the experience arising from the skill and success of our own planters, goes beyond that of all other nations; and if we consider their early improvements, and the vast extent to which they have been carried; and at the same time reflect, that these have been owing to no one circumstance more than to the smallness of their islands, which for the reasons that have been already given, enabled them to get the start and to keep it so long from the *French*, will abundantly satisfy every judicious and impartial inquirer, that what we have been

laying

laying down, is not more confiftent in fpeculation, than evident from the light of facts. Upon the whole therefore, we may look upon it as an abfolute certainty, that we fhall be gainers rather than lofers, from the fize of thefe iflands; and this difficulty removed, we may the more eafily comprehend, what, upon probable grounds, in reference to thefe new acquifitions we may have juft reafon to expect.

The faireft and the moft fatisfactory method that can be taken in refpect to this, is to compare them with our old poffeffions, the value of which is fo well known, and has been by our ableft writers fo often ftated. The new iflands taken all together, contain upon the moft moderate computation, twice the quantity of ground capable of cultivation, or at leaft very near it, that there is in *Barbadoes* and all the *Leeward Iflands*. *St. Vincent*, is not much inferior in fize to *Barbadoes*, and the reft are all confiderably larger. In refpect to their foil and climate, they are indifputably to the full as capable of improvement, as any of thofe that have been improved by our induftrious countrymen in fo high a degree. Why therefore in a reafonable fpace of time, may not we, or our pofterity at leaft, expect to derive twice as much from them?

Thefe new colonies, like our old colonies in that part of the world, muft depend entirely upon us, and draw from hence every neceffary, every conveniency that they want, either for their own subsistence, or for the carrying on of their plantations; and how extremely beneficial this is, and with so considerable an increase will be, to the mother country, has been already so amply explained, that it would be tedious as well as unnecessary to enter into any repetition here. It is requisite only to remark, that we shall not be obliged to wait for all, or even the greatest part of the benefits of this commerce, till such time as these islands are fully and compleatly settled, so as to vie in their productions with our old islands; but on the contrary, our exports to them, and of consequence the profits upon those exports, will very soon commence, and of course we shall immediately reap great advantages from them. The reason of this is obvious, for tho' our old colonies require annually many things, our new ones will require all; and it is easy to distinguish the difference that there must be, in supplying the vast variety of things requisite for settling new colonies, and the furnishing the annual subsistence, together with the wear and tear in the old ones. Nor is there any room to fear, that these new settlers will not find wherewithal to make very considerable returns, for though this cannot be at first done in sugar, yet in mahogany, cotton, and a great variety of other articles it may, and the very balance remaining a debt, will be a most effectual spur to industry, and compel the new planters, to work hard and to live frugally, as the original settlers in the other islands did,

did, in order to procure new supplies with that view, and to maintain and extend their credit.

This intercourse between the new colonies and their mother country, as it must from the causes before-mentioned begin early, so the advantages arising from it will diffuse themselves generally over the whole island of *Great Britain*; indeed thro' the whole sphere of the *British* dominions in *Europe*, since very large quantities of linnen and salt provisions, will be exported for the use of the new settlers and their servants, from *Ireland*; and in process of time, as they shall become more numerous, we may with great probability hope, their increased demands will, in a very great measure at least, absorb those supplies with which the inhabitants of that island have hitherto furnished the *French* and *Spanish* ships, and contributed thereby to their navigating much cheaper than otherwise they could have done; so that considered in this point of light, the inhabitants of the new colonies, will not only afford a fresh market to our fellow subjects in that island, but contribute at the same time to distress our *rivals* in the trade of the *West-Indies*.

But it is requisite farther to observe, in order to set the importance of these islands in a full light, that, exclusive of the benefits flowing from their direct trade with us, they will bring us likewise very considerable advantages, by the encouragement they will afford to other branches of our commerce. The *African* trade, more especially

especially at the beginning, will receive a new spring from their demands, since all that they can do either at present or in future, must arise from the labour of their *Negroes*. The supplying them with slaves therefore, will be both an instantaneous and a continual source of wealth, to such as are employed in that lucrative trade, more especially to those who have the largest share of it, the merchants of *London*, *Bristol*, and *Liverpool*.

We have before shewn, how this trade comes to be of such importance to *Great Britain*, as it is carried on principally with our own manufactures, and more especially with woollen goods of different kinds, to a very large amount, and that all the incidental profits, exclusive of what is produced by slaves, which arise from our correspondence with *Africa*, whether obtained by the purchase of elephants teeth and gold-dust, upon the coasts of that country, or from the sale of commodities to foreigners in the *West-Indies*, finds its way hither. On the winding up of the account therefore, as the sale of the *Negroes* centers in the *West-Indies*, the profit arising upon them, and every other accession of gain, from whatever article produced, centers ultimately here, and becomes the property of the inhabitants of *Britain*.

This will appear with the greater degree of evidence, when we reflect, that more than the moiety of that part of the cargo for the *African* trade, which is not made up of our own goods, consists confists of the manufactures of the *East-Indies*. It has been before observed, that besides the quantity of *India* goods employed on the coast of *Africa*; there is likewise no small demand for the same commodities in our old sugar colonies; and of course there will be the like demand in the new. We see from hence, how the comprehensive chain of commerce is united, and how the different products of the most distant parts of the world, are carried to and brought from these distant countries in *British* shipping; and that all the emoluments arising from this extensive navigation, is in the end the reward of the consummate skill, the indefatigable industry, and the perpetual application, of the traders in this happy isle, and how it is to be augmented and supported by this new accession of territory.

The prodigious compass of this commercial circulation, would be after all very defectively represented, if we should omit the mentioning the constant correspondence that subsists between the *sugar* islands and the *northern* colonies. A correspondence equally necessary, and reciprocally advantageous to those of our countrymen who are settled in both; and a correspondence therefore, which will be always maintained, and by which the numerous subjects of *Britain* who are seated on the continent of *America*, and those settled in the *West-India* islands, in pursuing their own immediate interests contribute, and contribute effectually to each others support.

support. This is a circumstance, that must fill the breast of every well-meaning man with the highest and most rational pleasure, and engage him to contemplate this subject, with a satisfaction, words would but faintly express, that kind of satisfaction, which warms the heart of a parent, when he sees his children assiduous in their application to those methods of providing for their welfare, which have a tendency to promoting their common interests, by which their harmony doubles the effects of their industry.

The *northern* colonies supply the *sugar* islands, chiefly with lumber and provisions. These are the fruits in a great measure of their indefatigable labour, and of their perpetual application to the rendering that labour subservient to their prosperity. By this means, they dispose of numerous bulky commodities, derive immense advantages from their fisheries, support an extensive navigation, which is so much the more profitable to them, as it is entirely carried on in ships of their own building; circumstances which, to the eye of a judicious reader, will place this trade, and all the beneficial consequences that attend it, in a very conspicuous point of view, and convince him that nothing can be either more convenient for these people, or more to their profit.

On the other hand, the benefits that result to the inhabitants of the sugar islands, are not less considerable. They draw all these necessary supplies from the nearest, and consequently from the cheapest markets, markets inexhaustible, and

and upon which they can always depend. These are brought them by their countrymen to their own doors, which is a circumstance exceedingly suitable to their situation, as it spares them the pains and labour requisite to provide them, which would be otherwise a great drawback on their industry, in their own plantations. These supplies they pay for in their own manufactures, which is another great advantage: from all which circumstances taken together, it clearly appears, that the convenience of this correspondence, and the benefits resulting from it, are equal on both sides, and exactly suited to the genius, temper, and situation of the people, by whom it is thus carried on.

By considering attentively this conjunction of interests, we cannot but plainly discern, that by these new acquisitions in the *West-Indies*, new markets are opened, to which our new subjects on the continent may resort. These islands will certainly in time more than replace to the people of *Canada* the trade they formerly carried on to the *French* colonies, and will at the same time enable our other settlements upon the continent, to find new customers for all their commodities, without leaving them that colour of necessity, which was the only excuse they had to plead, for supplying our rivals with the materials essentially requisite to their manufactures, and of course detrimental in the same degree, to those of our fellow subjects. Besides as the increase of our sugar islands affords

them

them this increase of commerce, so from their situation they will be a great bar to that illicit trade with the *French*, which cannot for the future be carried on with the same facility as before.

But the greatest advantage of all, and from which we were induced to dwell so long upon this subject, is the consideration of its effect. As the inhabitants of the sugar colonies, are continual purchasers from such as are settled upon the continent of *America*, the amount of their purchases constitutes a balance from them in the favour of all those who dispose of them. But on the other hand, the inhabitants of the northern colonies, drawing large and constant supplies of commodities and manufactures from hence, we for the same reason have a like balance in our favour against them. It is evident therefore from this deduction, that by their transferring the balance due to them, in satisfaction for that which is due from them to us, the whole accumulated profits of these transactions ultimately center with the inhabitants of *Great Britain*. Such are the certain, the perpetual, the prodigious benefits, that accrue to us from our PLANTATIONS.

There will be room in these new islands, for attempting many things, and improving more. The planting *cacao* walks cannot be considered as impracticable, since we see the *French* have succeeded in it, and so no doubt might we, at least in a degree sufficient to furnish our own consump-

consumption. We have *coffee* already in our islands, but it would certainly turn to more account, if the culture of it was better understood; in order to which some pains should be taken, to be thoroughly informed of the manner in which it is managed in *Arabia*, since it is not at all improbable, that the *flavour*, in which only our coffee is deficient, depends upon the culture, and the method of curing it. *Tea*, if we may believe the *French* is a native of the *West* as well as of the *East-Indies*, in respect to which it would be certainly right to make some inquiries, and in consequence of them some experiments; and if from thence it should appear it is not already there, it might be easily carried thither, and a trial might be as easily made whether it might not be cultivated to advantage.

It has been judged no difficult matter to introduce black *pepper*. *Rhubarb*, *senna*, and several other drugs, are said to have been raised by curious people in very great perfection. If the culture of these and other medicinal plants, was once well understood, they might be rendered profitable articles in commerce. The laudable society for promoting arts and manufactures, have given several premiums with respect to *sarsaparilla* and other things; and it is to be hoped, as well as wished, that these endeavours so well intended may have good effects. The increasing the number of our commodities appears to be a thing of consequence, even though they should not turn to immediate profit,

because

because they might serve as resources in succeeding times, in case of such alterations hapening hereafter as have already happened, in respect to what were long esteemed staple commodities.

The success attending these, or any other experiments of the like kind, might become the means of improving many spots of ground, that would otherwise prove useless, as it is well known that either lands worn out, or which are utterly unfit for either sugar or cotton, might be employed for the making of *cochineal*. The raising a variety of commodities would prevent the losses that ensue from short crops; as seasons unfavourable for some things, might be advantageous to others. Besides, in respect to many things that have been mentioned, the cultivation of them might be carried on with fewer *Negroes*, and yet afford a comfortable subsistence to white families, the increase of which (a thing wisely and constantly attended to by the *French*) in our colonies, is an object of great importance. Add to all this, that tho' *tea*, *coffee*, and *chocolate* are at present not improperly considered as articles of luxury, they would be much less so, if they only, or even if they principally came from our own plantations, and the consumption of them, should it become greater than it now is, would likewise promote and increase the consumption of our great staple commodity *sugar*. In these, and in various other lights, such improvements would

would be found of very great confequence, and are therefore extremely well worthy of confideration.

It will evidently appear from a due attention to thefe inconteftable facts, that our national interefts were ftudioufly confulted and fteadily purfued, in thus vindicating our claim to, and procuring the poffeffion of the neutral iflands. For by fettling thefe, we fhall at once obtain an acceffion of power and of wealth, the former of which would have been always precarious, if the inhabitants of iflands belonging to us in this part of the world, had not been the natural fubjects of the crown of *Great Britain*, and the latter would have been diminifhed, if in order to remedy that evil, we had laid out immenfe fums of ready money, in the purchafe of private property. On the contrary this nation will be immediately and continually gainers by all thefe new fettlements, from the very moment that our people enter upon them, becaufe from that very inftant they will ftand in need of fupplies from hence, more efpecially of *Negroes*, upon which their cultivations of every kind will neceffarily depend; and in the very fame proportion that thefe proceed and extend, the fupplies from the mother country and the northern colonies will continually augment, and their confequence will of courfe be more and more felt, and their importance from thence be the better underftood.

The settlement of these new islands, will be no detriment to our old colonies. It seems to to have been the only point, in which contending writers agree, that there was a real want of more sugar land in the *West-Indies*; and this being admitted, it would be a glaring absurdity to say, that *Britain* is not a great gainer by these acquisitions, which put so large a quantity of land fit for the cultivation of sugar into our possession. In reality, this was not only an opinion in respect to the truth of which the best judges agreed, but it was a point also decided from matter of fact. Because it is known that numbers of *British* subjects resorted to countries in the possession of other powers. It cannot be denied, that many *English* are settled in the *Danish* island of *St. Cruz*; that there are many resident in *Eustatia*; and that many more, are interested in the *Dutch* settlements upon the continent of *America*. It was therefore highly requisite to remove this evil, by giving such adventurers an opportunity of exercising their industry, in countries belonging to their mother country; and to these it is reasonable to presume, this opportunity being given them, they will return. Besides, as from these facts it appears, that our old colonies began to be over-stocked, so as to afford little encouragement to new planters, it was incumbent upon those who had the care of national affairs, to have an eye to this circumstance, in order to prevent such enterprizing people, as at any rate were determined to

seek

seek their fortunes in these parts, from being driven into foreign settlements, where their labour and industry, instead of being beneficial to us, would have turned to the advantage of our rivals, and foreign markets would have been supplied, for the profit of foreigners, by commodities which were raised, by the skill and pains of *British* subjects.

We may likewise see from hence, that there is no reason to apprehend, that these new islands will be a great, much less a dangerous, drain from this country. We cannot but observe from what has already happened, that people who are indigent here, would go in search of subsistence elsewhere; and we must be likewise sensible, that by providing countries for such people to resort to, their industry though not their persons will still be preserved to *Britain*. By that increase of trade which their labours abroad will gradually produce at home, the number of our necessitous people here will be greatly lessened. There will be larger quantities of our commodities and manufactures wanted, that are requisite in our plantations, and to supply these, numbers must be set to work, who are either now idle for want of it, and are subsisted by the poor's rate; or take methods of subsisting themselves, more injurious to the public, and much less to their own advantage, than if they betook themselves to honest labour here, or even went abroad to these new islands.

As

As the natural body increases in vigour, by assimilating wholesome food; so the strength of the body politic, is supported, by the proper direction of the labour and industry of its members; for idle persons are not only useless, but a burthen to the community. It has been fully proved, from the strongest and clearest reasons, and from the concurrent experience of more than a century, that the force of this nation has been augmented, and her grandeur heightened, by the advantages she has derived from her old colonies. It has been likewise shewn, that the like advantages may be certainly drawn from the new; that these will be universally beneficial to all parts of our *European* dominions; that they will afford employment to multitudes, who have it not at present; that they will enlarge our *African* and *East-India* as well as other foreign trades; that by increasing our navigation, they will give subsistance to our seamen; and that by an universal enlargement of our commercial efforts, they will not only gradually but speedily repair the wastes of war, promote the arts and blessings of peace, and contribute to fix the envied happiness of this nation, with the blessing of Divine Providence, in a higher degree of eminence, than was ever known before the reign of our present Sovereign, the indulgent Father of a brave, active, and loyal people.

www.ingramcontent.com/pod-product-compliance
Lightning Source LLC
Chambersburg PA
CBHW022009220426
43663CB00007B/1021